Bread of Life

First Communion Program

CARL J. PFEIFER
JANAAN MANTERNACH

Paulist Press New York, N.Y. / Ramsey, N.J.

CONTENTS

Introduction

Parent Consultants:
Sue and Vic Alessi
Sharon and Ray Connolly
Maureen Kelly
Pat and Bill Seiler
Peg and Ken Telesca

Library of Congress
Catalog Card Number: 78-70686

ISBN: 0-8091- 9539-9

Published by Paulist Press
Editorial Office: 1865 Broadway, New York, N.Y. 10023
Business Office: 545 Island Road, Ramsey, N.J. 07446

Printed and bound in the United States of America

Copyright © 1978 by The Missionary Society of St. Paul the Apostle in the State of New York

Nihil Obstat
Rev. James M. Cafone, S.T.L., M.A.
Censor Librorum

Imprimatur
Most Reverend Peter L. Gerety, D D.
Archbishop of Newark

November 3, 1978

Dear Parents,

Some friends of ours recently told us a story about themselves and their seven-year-old. While going through a serious crisis in their marriage, their problems have led to frequent and long-lasting conversations as they struggle to hold their marriage together. They were startled one day when Jason said to them, "You look so good together, when you are together." Their struggle is not yet over, but their young son gave them food for much thought and talking through.

Children are amazing creatures. They have surprising abilities, like memorizing names and averages of scores of athletes whose cards they have collected, or swimming like fish, or playing drums, or learning facts by the bushel and asking questions endlessly. But perhaps their greatest ability is along the lines Jason exemplified.

Children can *see* things and *feel* things that are really important, even though they rarely reveal their insights in words. A child tends to sense that what is really important may not be measurable and definable. Like the Little Prince, they know that "it is only with the heart that one can see rightly. What is essential is invisible to the eye."

That's why children *wonder* at things grown-ups rush right by. That's why they learn so much from good stories. They learn most and best from what they can hear, see, feel, and touch. Words help if they give a name to something that is experienced.

We believe that your child's First Communion preparation should build on his or her normal way of learning about what is important in life, and that it should respect what Communion really is. Communion is more to wonder at than to define. It is learned more by living into it than by analyzing it. Stories tell us more about it than abstract definitions do. It has to do with love, which you know from experience eludes precise rational categories. Communion is about God whose love for us is so incredible that he becomes one of us and shares food and drink with us.

Enjoy helping your child sense something of the wonder at what Communion is all about. We have tried to give you all the help you need regarding what to do and how to do it as well as why it should be done at home anyway. These weeks of preparation can be a really special time for you and the whole family. It matters not if you are a single parent or if you have a large family. You and your child, together with any other members of the family there may be at hand, have an opportunity to learn together about what it means to share in Communion.

Our concern is more with your experience than with your "teaching," although you will be teaching your best lessons through the experiences you have together. We feel that it is of greater value for you to share pictures and stories and symbols with your child than theological words, although the words you will use are profoundly theological.

This is not so much a course as a time of family sharing. We hope you enjoy it. If you do, there is a good chance your child will learn that Communion is a joyful reality. Receiving Communion for the first time may be just the start of years of sharing together Jesus' gift of himself as the Bread of Life. You have the opportunity to be sure that your child approaches Communion for the first time with the best preparation possible—that which *only you* as his or her parent can give.

We envy you. "You are so good together, when you are together."

Janaan and *Carl*

P.S. You might be interested in our answers on the next pages to questions many parents have asked us about First Communion.

QUESTIONS YOU MAY HAVE—MANY PARENTS DO

1. Why First Communion preparation?

Your child has probably been going to Mass with you for years. He or she may have had an introduction to the Eucharist as part of regular religion classes at school or CCD. Your child may even have received Communion already on occasion.

First Communion preparation need not be another introduction to the Eucharist as a whole, although it can recall and reinforce the main themes of the Eucharist. It is rather an opportunity to celebrate as a family and as a parish community an important step in your child's growth as a Christian. Communion is the full sharing in the sacrament that is the center of the Church's life. It is a special opportunity to become more closely united with Jesus Christ and with all his friends. The initiation process begun at baptism is completed as one fully joins the community at worship in eating the Bread of Life and drinking the cup of salvation. Your child is about to take that step. It is worth preparing for and celebrating together.

2. Why involve parents in First Communion preparation?

Preparing for First Communion is more a kind of initiation into a way of living than an academic or instructional experience. It is more like learning to eat or to love than learning a theory about eating or loving. That kind of learning happens best at home. Even if there are lessons in school or CCD for First Communion, the parents' attitude and involvement are critical to what the child really learns.

Then, too, parents have a *right* to share in something so important in their child's life and growth. You feed, clothe, shelter and provide "taxi" service for your children. You have a vital role in your child's religious growth as well, whether you are conscious of it or not. That influence may be positive or negative, but it is never neutral. The gift of faith to your child is God's to give. But the nurture of that gift goes on chiefly in the day-to-day living that goes on at home. Taking part in the First Communion preparation allows you to take a more active, positive part in encouraging your child's growth as a Catholic Christian.

3. What exactly will I as parent have to do?

Several important and for the most part rather simple and natural things will have to be done.

First of all, you will have a chance to enjoy with your child a family breakfast, lunch, dinner, picnic or walk, prayer time or party, and quiet time to plan a project to help someone. The Child's Book and these notes give you step-by-step directions and also provide the basic resources you will need. Planning these six family gatherings should take you less than half an hour each.

The most important things you will have to do are things you probably want to do anyway— try to grow closer together as a family, enjoy each other and your life together more, deepen your own appreciation for Communion, and get to know and love Jesus Christ better.

4. What should characterize First Communion preparation at home?

Naturalness is one important thing. You are not asked to turn your home into either a classroom or a chapel. You don't have to become a professional teacher or priest, theologian or expert. You are to be a parent, sharing your ideas and feelings, your faith, about something you have done that your child is about to do for the first time.

Enjoyment is also very important. Some might prefer to use words like joy or fun. You and your child should really enjoy being together as you eat, look at pictures, read poems, tell stories, perhaps take a walk, have a picnic or party, and talk about your lives together and communion.

Prayer, too, is important—not in any overly formal, structured sense, but more in a sense, at times expressed in words or songs, that you are aware of Christ's presence and the Father's goodness. The Child's Book and this book will give you practical helps along the way.

5. What is my responsibility in the First Communion preparation?

As a mother or father you have the *primary responsibility* for preparing your child for First Communion. You, first of all, also have the *right* to do so.

This involves deciding when you feel your child is ready for First Communion. It also means helping him or her learn the minimum essentials and acquire a desire for Communion.

Yours is the first right and responsibility, but you are not alone. Your parish priest, your child's religion teacher, the parish director of religious education, and other parents who are also preparing children for First Communion can all help you.

Most probably your parish will have one or more meetings planned to help you understand your role and appreciate your responsibility. The Director's Book gives concrete suggestions for three parish meetings and three parish celebrations.

6. What does my child have to know before First Communion?

Your parish may have its own set of requirements for First Communion. You can learn these by calling the pastor or another priest at the rectory or the director of religious education. Usually they are explained in the church bulletin or special announcements.

The Church's general requirements are very simple and have been very much the same since the Middle Ages. A child must have the ability to distinguish the Eucharist from ordinary bread and have a desire to receive it. We might say it another way. *Children must know that the bread and wine received in Communion are more than ordinary bread and wine, and they must want to receive Communion.* To do that they need no detailed theology of the Eucharist or of the basic doctrines of the Church. *Such awareness does imply some simple awareness of Jesus, who he is, and that he is with us. It also includes at least an awareness of God our Father who loves us each very much and cares for us.* All that is needed is a *child's* knowledge of Communion as a *meal with Jesus.* Keep in mind that your child does not need to know all that you have realized about Communion over the years.

You need not worry that your child is perhaps not learning many of the questions and answers you may have had to learn as a child before First Communion. These are simply not required.

The BREAD OF LIFE program contains much more than the minimum requirements. Actually much of what was in the older question-answer preparations is included in BREAD OF LIFE in different language—language more attuned to a child's way of thinking and to the Gospels and liturgy.

7. Who decides when my child is ready?
Again, parishes may have different practices. But the ordinary practice of the Church at large has also come down from the Middle Ages. Those who decide are those who know the child best. Practically, this means that the child's parents are the ones to make the decision. It is their right as parents. Because First Communion involves a step that also involves the parish community, the priest is normally involved in a consultative role, assisting the parents in their decision. In today's parishes the teachers and parish religious education directors are normally also very helpful to parents in this matter.

8. What is the earliest my child may go to Communion?
Your child has the right to go to Communion as soon as he or she meets the basic requirements mentioned above. For a child in a Catholic family that practices its faith, this means simply that your child (1) knows that the eucharistic food is more than ordinary food, and (2) desires to receive it. Whatever his or her age, anyone who knows that and wants to go to Communion may be allowed to do so. You may, however, have good reasons for wanting your child to wait a bit longer.

9. What about first confession before First Communion?
Because of the diversity of practice throughout the United States and the Church as a whole, you should check what is the normal practice in your diocese and parish. According to general Church law no one has a right to prevent your child from Communion if the above-mentioned conditions are met. Confession before Communion is required of Catholics of all ages *only* when they are conscious of deliberately committing a mortal sin. You may rest assured that your child does not have the ability to sin mortally, certainly if he or she is younger than ten or twelve. Therefore confession is not required before a child's First Communion. However in your parish or diocese it may be the practice, and if done sensitively it may benefit your child.

10. What should my child wear for First Communion?
Customs vary from parish to parish. If your parish has no set practice, you may have your child wear whatever seems most appropriate to you. What he or she wears should include something special to add to the awareness that this is a special occasion for all of you. White suit and tie or white dress and veil may have real meaning for you and your child because of past associations. Remember that you are free in this matter. What your child wears is important, but it should not become more important than the reception of Communion itself.

11. How should my child receive—in the hand or on the tongue?
Every Catholic is free to receive in either way. Your child has the right to receive either in the hand or on the tongue. Your child's book shows how to receive in either way (see pages 114-115).

It is good to give your child a chance to practice receiving Communion several times beforehand. Your priest or parish religious education director can provide bread similar to that used in your parish for the Eucharist. If your child receives under both species, bread and wine, be sure to let him or her taste some wine several times before receiving Communion.

12. In using the BREAD OF LIFE program to prepare my child for First Communion, how should I begin?

Relax! Look forward to these weeks as pleasant, enjoyable times of family experiences and learning.

Think about your own First Communion. Remember what you liked, what meant something to you. Also be aware of what you found painful, what you did not like. You may learn from your own experience what you might like to do or avoid.

Take a few minutes to page through the beautiful BREAD OF LIFE book you will be giving to your child. Try to get a feel for it. See how delightful it is, how special, how filled with photographs, art, illustrations, story, poetry and song about Communion and about what Communion has to do with our daily lives. It is meant to be a delightful book that your child may cherish long after First Communion day. It has a "keepsake" kind of quality. It says more about the feelings, approach, and attitudes you may want to create in your home as you prepare your child for First Communion than any further explanations.

Alongside of your child's book, look through this, your book. Read the rest of the Introduction to get an idea of what is to be experienced and learned by your child.

Explanations of the various words used to describe this sacrament—Mass, Eucharist, etc.—are found on page 13.

A chart giving an overview of the whole BREAD OF LIFE program is on page 15. It is preceded by a brief explanation of the six session themes. You may find these helpful in understanding just what is in the program and what you will be sharing with your child.

The page with Features and Benefits, pages 16-18, may also be helpful to you.

Records of the songs recommended in the various sessions are also available. These can be very helpful in adding a joyful note of song to the preparation.

Notice that each session gives you:
(a) *Just a thought*—a brief explanation of the session;
(b) *A Plan of Action*—the step-by-step plan to guide you;
(c) *Background Notes*—more extended notes about the session to help you understand something of its theological basis.

Finally, Pray to the Holy Spirit to guide you in what is a privilege and may be a pleasure.

MANY NAMES, ONE REALITY

During the many centuries since the Last Supper the Church has called the meal recalling the Last Supper by many names. Several names are still used by Roman Catholics and other Christians. Here are a few of them and their meanings. The variety of names suggests something of the richness of this sacrament.

1. MASS.
Most of us probably grew up familiar with the word "Mass." It has been the typical Roman Catholic term since the Reformation in the sixteenth century. Before that "Mass" was used by the Church in the West (as opposed to the Eastern Churches) for some centuries. The name comes from the Latin word *missa* (remember *Ite, missa est?*) Its original meaning seems to have been "sent with a blessing," from the final blessing and dismissal. But "Mass" gradually came to mean the whole eucharistic celebration.

2. LITURGY.
In the East the traditional name for the Mass has been "Liturgy" or "Sacred Liturgy." It remains the normal term in Orthodox Churches and the Oriental rites of the Roman Catholic Church. This word has a very long history. "Liturgy" comes from the Greek word for "work of service," used originally for works of public service in the Greek cities. The term has connotations of something the people, the community, do. When used in the Roman Catholic Church "liturgy" usually refers to the entire official public worship of the Church, particularly the sacraments.

3. LORD'S SUPPER.
This terminology is still used by many Protestant Christian churches. It goes all the way back to St. Paul's writings to the church at Corinth (1 Cor. 11:20). The name more clearly relates to the fact that the sacramental meal is related to the Last Supper and is a meal shared with the risen Lord.

4. COMMUNION.
Holy Communion is also a commonly used Protestant title for the service which includes the taking of Communion. The term stresses the aspect of community arising from eating and drinking together in memory of the Lord. In Roman Catholic usage "Communion" or "Holy Communion" refers to one part of the whole eucharistic celebration rather than to the whole service.

5. EUCHARIST.
From the Greek word for "thanksgiving" or "praise" this ancient word has recently become common in Roman Catholic usage. It refers to the entire celebration and is now a frequent alternative for "Mass." It also refers to the second major section of the celebration, the liturgy of the Eucharist, which follows the liturgy of the word. "Eucharist" suggests the attitude of one who is aware of receiving a great gift: thanksgiving and praise. This was a common name for the celebration in the early Church.

6. BREAKING OF BREAD.

Rarely used today, this is perhaps the most common name for the eucharistic meal in the New Testament itself. It refers directly to Jesus' action of breaking bread at the Last Supper. This symbolic action is still retained as part of the Communion rite of the Eucharist.

AN OVERVIEW OF THE BREAD OF LIFE PROGRAM

SESSION	THEME	LIFE EXPERIENCE	FAMILY SETTING	GOSPEL STORY	DOCTRINAL BASE
1	Invitation	Being special	Dinner	Last Supper Mark 14 Matthew 26 Luke 22	Institution by Christ
2	Presence	Being with	Picnic or walk	Emmaus walk and meal Luke 24	Real Presence
3	Unity	Being together	Breakfast	Seashore breakfast John 21	Sacrament of Unity
4	Food	Eating	Lunch	Feeding of 5,000 + Bread of Life John 6	Eucharist as Meal (Transubstantiation)
5	Gift	Gift-giving	Prayer time or party	Last Supper and Cross Luke 22	Eucharist as Sacrifice
6	Service	Helping	Quiet time for planning	Footwashing John 13	Sacrament of Love

The experience and theme of Thanksgiving weaves through all the sessions.

THE BREAD OF LIFE program involves six family sessions at home that deal with the meaning of Communion. The six sessions do not go through the entire structure of the Eucharist. This is normally done as part of the regular religious education program in parochial school and CCD. Rather the six sessions *focus on Communion*, while drawing on *important themes from the whole Mass*, particularly the liturgy of the Eucharist.

The program is a preparation for *First Communion*, but it does not take Communion out of the context of the whole Eucharist, as was at times done in earlier years through an exaggerated emphasis on the Communion experience. You might find the outline of the Eucharist in general and the Communion rite in particular helpful. Look at pages 112-113 of the Child's Book.

The themes of the six sessions may each be stated in one word: *Invitation, Presence, Community, Food, Gift, Service. Thanksgiving* is a theme that runs through all the sessions, reflecting the attitude of Jesus. Each time he took bread and gave it to his friends, he thanked God his Father. The name "Eucharist" means "thanksgiving."

The approach to the various themes is always in terms of ordinary *life experience*. This is not just because children learn best from concrete experiences. It is also theologically important. Communion is about life. It celebrates Jesus' presence with us not just in the Eucharist but in daily life. It is the sign and source of unity not just as we worship together but in our families and neighborhoods. Communion is the Bread of *Life*.

In each session a *Gospel story* provides the bridge between the life experience and the Eucharist. We want the children to relate Communion with *Jesus*. Jesus is not visible at Mass. He is not tangible in Communion. But through the Gospel stories the child can associate Jesus with his or her life and with the Eucharist. By entering into the Gospel story the children may gradually associate Jesus with Communion in a more moving way. Each of the Gospel stories is authentically about the Eucharist, about Communion. What is described in the Gospel takes place today in the Eucharist. The adapted versions of the Gospel text in the child's BREAD OF LIFE book stress this tie between the Gospel event and the Mass. In the Gospels these stories actually reflect the practices of the early Christian communities as they celebrated the Lord's supper in their homes.

The *doctrinal base* underlies the development of each lesson. But the language used in the accompanying chart to identify the doctrinal basis of each session is not used with the children. The children need not learn abstract theological words. In the session, more simple, concrete language and symbols are used to say what the more difficult language of theology expresses abstractly.

The *family settings* are selected to fit in as naturally as possible with the theme of each session and the Gospel story involved. Family learning about Communion in typical settings reflecting ordinary family life can make the learning much more natural and real for the child, and for the whole family as well. Communion preparation is not just a matter of learning information about Communion. It is much more a learning together of fundamental Christian attitudes and an authentically Catholic Christian way of life.

FEATURES AND BENEFITS

The BREAD OF LIFE program is characterized by certain features that involve benefits to the adults and children involved in the First Communion preparation.

1. FAMILY CENTERED.

The most effective place for children to prepare for First Communion is at home with their whole family. Naturally the family needs to be assisted and supported by the parish as a whole. BREAD OF LIFE places the greatest emphasis on the family preparation at home, while providing resources for the parish and the school or CCD to aid the families. The sessions involving the whole family are set within the context of general family life. It is suggested that the family session be followed up by a review session between parents and the child.

2. PARISH CENTERED.

First Communion is the personal experience of a child who is part of a family, which is part of the local parish community. First Communion is the final step in the gradual initiation of someone into full communion with the local worshiping community, the parish. So First Communion is a parish celebration as well as a family and personal celebration. BREAD OF LIFE provides for parish *instructional* sessions and parish *celebrations* to help parents and teachers prepare their children for what is meant to be a parish community experience.

3. LIFE ORIENTED.

First Communion preparation is not just about Communion. It is about life, particularly life lived as a Catholic Christian. So BREAD OF LIFE from beginning to end deals with daily experiences of life. The sessions at home are designed to take place in typical family experiences—meals, quiet time, picnic or party, prayer time, and project planning time. The themes rest on the experiences of being present with another, being united with others, gift-giving, eating, and helping. Communion is an integral part of life for a Christian.

4. BALANCED THEOLOGICALLY.

The program draws upon the most ancient traditions as well as the most recent teachings and practices of the Church regarding the Eucharist. It is rich in stories from the Gospels that deal with the Eucharist. It provides ancient and more modern prayers that are related to the Eucharist. It draws upon the prayers and symbols of the eucharistic liturgy, particularly those surrounding Communion itself.

5. NATURAL.

Insofar as possible, all learning about Communion in this program takes place in settings that are natural to both child and parents, e.g., around a table, in the living room or kitchen, around the fireplace, at a favorite picnic place or in the backyard or at a local restaurant. The instructional content is placed ''up front'' in the sessions to suit what is perhaps more natural or peculiar to children. It needs to be attacked quickly and completely *before* eating or snacking, walking or popping corn. Sessions of children and catechist are designed to be informal and natural whether held at home or in school.

6. SIMPLE.
Simplicity was strived for in the structure of the entire program. Only one main point is covered in each session. The single point is approached from an experience of the child and family (e.g., being together at a special breakfast), a Gospel story that is eucharistic (e.g., the disciples together on the seashore eating breakfast with each other and with Jesus), and Communion today (e.g., at Communion we are united with Jesus and his friends). Detailed step-by-step directions are given all along the way. The sessions are lined up so that they simply follow the pages in the child's book, one after the other.

7. DELIGHTFUL.
An overriding concern of the authors and the publisher is that those who are using this program to prepare for a First Communion event should find it a delightful, enjoyable and rewarding experience. The book for the child was designed with an intent to make it something special, with imaginative art, creative photography, original poetry, traditional and contemporary prayers, playful but meaningful songs and spaces for a child to insert himself or herself.

Everything that we know about the meaning of eucharistic Communion suggests that it be a harmonious, joyous, wonderful and enriching experience of "being with." Therefore, the moments that are spent by a family in preparing for Communion should not be a time which is burdensome, boring, and creative of tension.

8. FLEXIBLE AND CREATIVE.
While every session is carefully worked out to provide step-by-step directions, the approach is such that the plan begs to be adapted. Your own creativity is encouraged. But there is no need to do anything more than what is laid out in the plans if they work reasonably well for you.

9. PRAYERFUL.
Prayer is encouraged at every stage of the preparation. Various forms of prayer are suggested. Prayers are provided from a variety of sources. Prayerful songs are included. BREAD OF LIFE is created to help you and your child grow not just in Catholic knowledge but in Catholic spirituality. First Communion preparation is seen as helping all who are involved in it grow in living out what Communion is all about, as well as helping a child get ready to receive Communion for the first time.

10. MULTI-SITUATIONAL.
The program can be used in several different ways depending on the needs and desires of parishes and parents. BREAD OF LIFE may be used in programs that are organized, for example, for the learning sessions to take place:
(a) *only at home*, with some support and guidance from the parish religious education personnel;
(b) *only in classes*, at school or CCD, with cooperation and support from home;
(c) *at home and classes*, either primarily the home with reinforcement sessions with a catechist in classes, or primarily in classes, with some followup sessions at home.

Whatever the home-classes balance, it is vital that at points the broader parish community be involved. There should be both *instructional sessions and parish celebrations.*

The following chart suggests the *ideal* way of using BREAD OF LIFE in a parish. However the program may be used successfully with a wide variation of adaptations.

(1) FAMILY SESSION	(2) PARENT FOLLOW- UP SESSION	(3) CLASS	(4) PARISH SESSIONS
The whole family uses the plan in the *Parent's Book* at a meal or other suggested family experience.	One or both parents meet quietly with the child alone to review and reinforce what was learned at the family session.	The children meet with the catechist for class in the school or CCD using the plan in the *Catechist's Book*	Parents and catechists meet two or three times for *instructional sessions* with the religious education minister or priest. All meet with the children two or three times for *celebrations*. Both kinds of parish sessions use plans in the *Director's Book*.

11. SENSITIVE TO VARYING AGES.

It is increasingly common for children of widely differing ages to be receiving First Communion. In many parishes children as old as twelve are preparing for First Communion, as are larger numbers of six-year-olds. BREAD OF LIFE attempts to provide for this broad spectrum of ages in its sensitive use of visual materials that do not limit interest to just very young children, and in its session plans which allow for great adaptation within their sound structure.

1. INVITATION
A Special Meal With Jesus

JUST A THOUGHT

It's good at times to feel special. It's a healthy feeling. In a world of increased depersonalization it's an important feeling.

Every child has a need to feel special. All children need to feel that they are important just because they are alive. Children need to feel important to themselves and to others. Actually every child is someone special, uniquely blessed and gifted. But many children seldom *feel* how special they are.

First Communion preparation can give you a chance to help your child feel like the special person he or she is. It is important for your child. It is also important for helping him or her grasp what Communion is all about.

Communion is something special. It is a meal with Jesus. To be invited to share this meal with Jesus and his friends is an honor. To be invited suggests that your child is important to Jesus and to those who love him or her. Your child is invited because he or she has something to bring to the community of Jesus' friends that no one else has. The meal is special. So are those who are invited.

That is really the main realization you want to help your child grasp during this first session. The fact that the Eucharist is a meal with Jesus is suggested by the story of the Last Supper. The central words and actions of the priest at Mass are the same as those of Jesus at the Last Supper. Communion is a meal with Jesus as much as the Last Supper was. The story of the Last Supper can help your child more easily see Communion as a meal with Jesus.

That's why First Communion is special and why anyone invited to the Communion meal with Jesus is a very special person.

A PLAN OF ACTION

Goal
To help your child:
(1) feel special, invited and welcomed to Communion by you and others who are important to him or her;
(2) learn that Communion is a meal with Jesus;
(3) that the very first Communion ever was at the Last Supper.

Experience
A special dinner, supper or another setting of your choice. Select a setting that your family finds natural for celebrating important family events. The plan suggests a special dinner or supper because of the focus on Communion as a meal with Jesus. Feel free to adapt it to your preference.

Materials
(1) Your child's BREAD OF LIFE book, and gift wrap for it.
(2) The BREAD OF LIFE record, and a record player.
(3) Room and table decorations
(4) Your child's favorite foods.

Preparations
(1) Read the plan below and adapt it to your family's style. See also the Background Notes on pages 24-27.
(2) Prepare the Child's Book to be given as a gift. Paste a recent photo of your child on page 15. On pages 18-19 fill in the remaining information on the invitation, and get as many to sign the invitations as possible—e.g., teachers, priests, godparents, neighbors, friends. Wrap the Child's Book in gift wrap.
(3) With the rest of the family, prepare small gifts that symbolize what each feels is special about the First Communion child. Wrap them decoratively. Or ask each to write a sincere compliment and place it in an envelope with the child's name on it.

Summary
(a) Using the Child's Book, talk together about being special and invited to Communion, a special meal with Jesus.
(b) Enjoy the dinner or supper together.
(c) Pray and sing at the end of the meal, using the Child's Book and record.

Directions

1. SHARE YOUR PLAN
Tell your child that you are going to begin the preparation for his/her First Communion by having a special meal. Build up some anticipation and excitement by showing how everything is decorated for the meal and that his or her favorite foods are on the menu. Indicate genuine happiness about the child's First Communion.

2. GIVE GIFTS
Sometime before the meal give your First Communion child the gifts or compliments that have been prepared by the family. As each gift is opened, the givers might say a few words about how the gift symbolizes something they feel is special about the child preparing for Communion.

Then give your child the Child's Book decorated with gift wrap. Tell him or her that it is something very special from the whole family for First Communion. Take a few moments to look at and talk about the book together.

Try to make the gift-giving a genuinely happy time so that your child senses how special to all of you he or she is.

3. TALK ABOUT BEING SPECIAL
The Child's Book may be helpful as you focus still more on what is special about your child. Use the book insofar as it helps him or her sense something of how special an event First Communion is. But do not let it become an obstacle to spontaneously talking and sharing.

The poem may be an enjoyable way of exploring your child's uniqueness. Read and talk about it. Your child may talk about his or her age, height, and special qualities now, but the information might be recorded in the book at another time. The brief prayer of St. Augustine expresses a healthy Christian self-appreciation.

1. INVITATION

Communion:
A Special Meal
with Jesus

Call your child's attention to the invitation and the signatures. They may help him or her feel something of how special the event is to so many people dear to him or her. Talk about the various people. Point out the First Communion date. Mark it on a calendar.

4. TALK ABOUT THE LAST SUPPER

Help your child to see that Communion is like the Last Supper, a meal with Jesus, and this is what makes it special. The Child's Book gives pictures of the Last Supper and a simplified version of the story. Look at the pictures together and talk about what each says. After looking at the pictures someone might read the story aloud. Or, together you may be able to recall most of the story just from the details of the pictures.

Draw attention in the pictures and story to Jesus, his disciples, the bread and wine, and Jesus' actions and words as he thanked God for the bread and wine and then gave them to the disciples. Ask your child if he or she has ever heard those words before or seen anyone doing almost the same thing as Jesus did. These are almost exactly the same words and actions of the priest at Mass. The priest does this in Jesus' name.

The Last Supper was the very first Communion ever. Just as the disciples shared a meal with Jesus, so do we at Communion. Communion is a special meal with Jesus.

Use the two pictures—Last Supper and Communion—to help your child see how similar the two meals are. Like the Last Supper, Communion is the *"Lord's supper."*

5. ENJOY THE MEAL

Relax now. You have helped your child learn something very important about himself or herself and about Communion. Now just celebrate the child and the special moment by enjoying the meal together.

Try to make this a memorable meal. Share with your child your memories of your First Communion—when and where it was, who was there, how you felt, what you wore and anything special that happened. Share any particular family or ethnic traditions about Communion that were part of your growing up. If you have other children, they might like to recall their First Communion memories too. If grandparents and other relatives are in the vicinity, they might share in the meal and share their experiences of Communion.

6. PRAY AND SING

At the end of the meal, take a few moments to pray and, if possible, to sing together. The Child's Book provides a beautiful "Prayer of Someone Special." Pray it together. Then sing or at least listen to the playful song. Try singing along with the record. It says how special everyone is.

WHAT TO DO DURING THE WEEK

To continue informally the preparation for First Communion begun at the special meal or other setting that you chose, you might do a few things like these

1.   Sit down with your First Communion child sometime during the week and go over the first session in the Child's Book. Help your child fill in the personal sketch on page 16. You might want your child to memorize a summary of what you have learned together, using the questions and answers on page 110. Questions 1-3 relate to this session. They are:

(1) Why is First Communion a special moment?
First Communion is a special moment because Jesus is with me in a new way for the first time. It is special because it is the first time I share fully in the Eucharist with my family, friends and parish community.

(2) What is Communion?
Communion is an important part of the Eucharist. Communion is sharing the Bread of Life, Jesus' gift of himself to us. Communion is being united with Jesus and with everyone who eats the Bread of Life.

(3) When was the very first Communion?
At the Last Supper Jesus gave himself to his friends as the Bread of Life for the first time. That was the very first Communion ever.

2. Copy out or help your child copy out the "Prayer of Someone Special" on pages 26-27. Hang it on the refrigerator door or someplace else where the whole family will notice it. Pray it together at mealtime or at bedtime all week.

3. Learn the song "Everybody has a Song" on pages 28-29 by heart. Sing it with your children occasionally during the week, or just play the recording of it from time to time.

4. Ask your child to write a personal prayer expressing his or her feelings about First Communion and desire to receive Communion. He or she could pray it sometime each day this week and modify it in weeks to come as Communion time gets closer.

5. Begin talking with your child about concrete plans for the First Communion celebration. Who will be invited? What kind of celebration do you all want? Where will it be? What time? What kind of clothes will your child wear for First Communion? (See the practical questions and answers on pages 9-12 of this book.)

6. Depending upon time and your personal feelings about "homemade" things, you may enjoy and find meaningful making invitations with your child for the people who will be invited to celebrate the First Communion event with your family and also making placemats for the occasion.

7. Plan the menus with your child for the meal(s) that you will eat at home on the First Communion day. If done decoratively, the child may want to keep them on display in his or her room.

BACKGROUND NOTES

A Warm Welcome

Children who are to receive Communion for the first time deserve a warm welcome. They may have been going to Mass for several years with their parents and teachers. but this will be the first time they can participate completely in the eucharistic meal. It is an important moment not just for the children and their families but for the whole parish community as well.

Sharing in Communion is a more complete sharing in the life and worship of the family and the community. It is through the community, particularly the family, that Jesus welcomes the children to full sharing in the Eucharist.

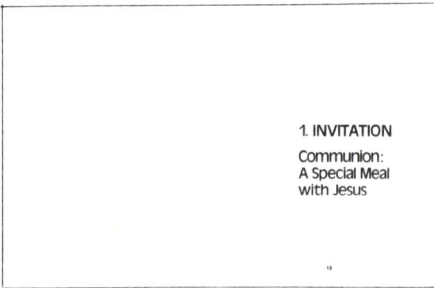

1. INVITATION

Communion:
A Special Meal
with Jesus

A Special Person

One of the finest ways to make children feel genuinely welcome is to help them feel appreciated as special persons. First Communion preparation is an ideal time for heightening their awareness of how unique and lovable each one is. Their gifts have been given to them by a loving God to be developed for their own joy and the joy of others. In becoming more fully a part of the community through their First Communion they bring their unique blend of gifts to share with and enrich the community. Each really is someone very special.

Part of First Communion preparation is to help the children discover and appreciate their unique beauty and value. It is as important to celebrate the child as it is to celebrate the First Communion event. Each communicant is a sign of what Communion is all about—the body of Christ which is the community of people, some old, some new, who continue to remember Jesus and to be his loving presence in the world.

An Invitation

A concrete sign of a person's value is an invitation to share in something important. An invitation is a gracious recognition of a person's importance to those inviting. The invitation to Communion should be warm and genuine. The signatures of parents, friends, neighbors, parish priest, teachers, godparents, relatives, and representatives of various parish groups symbolize their personal invitation to each First Communicant. Hopefully at least some could extend their invitation even more meaningfully than just signing the children's books.

If the invitation to the children reveals bonds of love between themselves and others in the community, it reveals what the Eucharist really is. Communion is not merely a private matter; it is a community experience. According to Catholic tradition and biblical teaching, the Eucharist is a sacrament of love, a sign and source of community. At the center and heart of the community is Jesus Christ.

The Very First Communion Ever

On the night before he died Jesus gathered his friends together for what was to be his final meal with them before he died. It was a time when he

St. Augustine was one of the great Fathers of the Church. He lived and wrote in Africa around 400 AD. The quotation is from his famous book, *Confessions*.

Note: Try to have as many people who are important to your child as possible sign the book.

Fill in the proper dates and the child's name.

spoke openly of his love for them. He urged them to love one another as he loved them. He prayed that they might grow in unity. The memory of him was to bind them together. The breaking of bread and sharing wine together in his name was to be a sign of his real presence with them always. Catholic teaching has long looked to the Last Supper as the time when Jesus instituted the sacrament of the Eucharist. The Last Supper was the very first Communion ever. The Gospel stories of that meal with Jesus are a touchstone for our understanding of the Eucharist as a whole and Communion in particular.

A Very Ancient Story
The story of the Last Supper is found at least five times in the New Testament. Paul gives the earliest account on record. Mark, Matthew and Luke tell much the same story as Paul, but all four differ slightly on details. John's account differs considerably.

The broad outlines of the biblical story of the Last Supper reveal that the words, actions and symbols of the Eucharist and the Last Supper are the same. The children can be helped to see the similarity between the Last Supper and the Eucharist. In this way they may come to believe that Communion is something more than eating ordinary food. It is a special meal, a meal they and their friends share with Jesus. To recognize this fact and to want to receive Communion are the minimum requirements for First Communion.

Memories Relived
Placing an artist's image of Jesus breaking bread at the Last Supper next to a photo of people receiving Communion visually suggests the similarity between the two experiences. From the earliest days of Christianity, when groups of friends "broke bread" together in private homes, down through the centuries, in every corner of the earth, men and women have continued to gather for the eucharistic meal. They recall what Jesus said and did at the Last Supper, in words and gestures similar to his.

As Catholics we believe that Communion is more than an act of remembering Jesus. We believe that the risen Lord is actually with us as we eat and

Note: Sources of the story:
Paul: 1 Cor. 11:23-26
Mark: 14:12-31
Matthew: 26:17-35
Luke: 22:7-38
John: 13-17

drink together the signs of his presence. We believe in his real presence with us, as real as his presence with his disciples at the Last Supper. We, and the children making their First Communion, have every reason to celebrate because we are called to the Lord's supper. It is a very special meal.

Somebody Special

And we have reason to celebrate because God our Father has graced us in so many other ways besides. In the Eucharist we thank and praise God for all his gifts, all of which we receive through Jesus Christ. For the children about to approach Communion for the first time, it is important that they discover still more how special they are as individuals. Psalm 139, the prayer here, expresses a deep sense of relationship with a wonderful God who has made each of us wonderful. The song *Everybody Has a Song* gives musical affirmation to the gift and possibility that each person has.

While Jesus invites all to faith in him and Communion with him, the actual acceptance of his invitation is a time for rejoicing in the fact that Jesus is inviting ME to his table. Jesus wants those who approach Communion to be aware of how loved they are, how beautiful and worthwhile they are. That's why our preparation for First Communion begins and ends with celebrating how special each child is. It is a time for praising and thanking God for his love which makes us lovable. Eucharist means "thanksgiving," "praise."

2. PRESENCE
At Communion Jesus Is With Us

JUST A THOUGHT

Joan was angry and hurt. "When is the last time you or Mom took some time just to be with me? I know you're busy. But what about me?" She began to cry.

Joan's experience is not unusual. We live in a busy world, filled with pressures. We have our own worries and problems. Time always seems to outrun us. Even in a family where we live so physically close to one another, it can happen that we are seldom really *with* one another. Presence is not just physical closeness.

This lesson is designed to give you an opportunity to *be with* your child in an enjoyable way. The idea is to take time, as part of First Communion preparation, to be *present to* your child, with no telephones, no business interruptions.

Perhaps it will take the form of a family picnic, or a walk with a snack at the end, or popcorn popping in the kitchen or around the fireplace, or just some quiet time together.

That kind of experience of being present can help your child make more sense of Jesus' presence with us. As Catholics we believe that Jesus is present in the Eucharist. He is with us at Communion. We also believe that he is with us at all times and in every place. The Mass celebrates his presence with us everywhere. Communion can help us to be more conscious of Jesus' presence.

But "real presence" may remain just an abstract idea for your child unless he or she has experiences of your caring presence, not just in this one lesson, but as a steady part of your family life.

A PLAN OF ACTION

Goal

To help your child to:
(1) have a good time with you, enjoying your presence;
(2) believe that Jesus is really present with us at Communion;
(3) believe that Jesus is really present with us always

Experience

A picnic, or a walk and snack, or similar experience like eating popcorn around the fireplace or in the kitchen. Do what your family tends to enjoy. What is important is that it is something that allows you to *be with* your child in a pleasant setting.

Materials

(1) The Child's Book.
(2) The record and record player.
(3) Food and drink that fits the setting you choose.

Preparations

(1) Read the plan below and adapt it to your family's style. See also the Background Notes on pages 33-36.
(2) Decide on the best setting.
(3) Prepare the food and drink.

Summary

(a) Talk together about presence, and Jesus' presence in the Eucharist, using the Child's Book.
(b) Enjoy the experience of presence together.
(c) Pray and sing together afterward, using the Child's Book and record.

Directions

1. SHARE YOUR PLAN

Tell your child and the rest of the family that you would like to do something they all might enjoy. Tell them you want to take some time just to be with them. Mention your plan for a picnic, or walk, or popcorn popping, so that they will have something to look forward to.

2. TALK ABOUT PRESENCE

Then talk together about being present to one another. Think out loud together about what a difference it makes when someone we love is really with us. Talk about the fun there is when we are with someone we care about.

Draw on the family's experience. Talk about times they felt a loved one's absence, such as when Mom or Dad went on a business trip, or when a playmate moved away, or when grandparents left after a visit. Then talk about times they felt the same person's presence, such as when Mom or Dad or the playmate or grandparents came back. Talk about how good it is to be with one another right now.

Use the Child's Book insofar as you find it a help to sharing about presence.

The poem and pictures may give leads to a variety of experiences your child has had of people's presence.

Talk as long as your child and others in the family are interested. Do not let concern for conversation or learning facts interfere with the experience of just being with your child and family.

3. TALK ABOUT A GOSPEL STORY

Build now on the family's experiences. Help them believe with you that Jesus is present with us all the time and in a special way at Communion.

Use the pictures of the Emmaus story and the written version of it insofar as it is helpful to you. You might show the pictures to your child and others in the family and simply tell the story in your own words, pointing out details in the picture as the story unfolds. Or maybe your family already knows the story and can tell it to you, using the picture.

As you talk together, point out what a difference Jesus' presence made to the two men. They were sad because Jesus was no longer with them. Then they felt better as the traveler walked with them and talked about the Scriptures. Finally they were overjoyed when, as he broke bread with them, they recognized him as their friend Jesus.

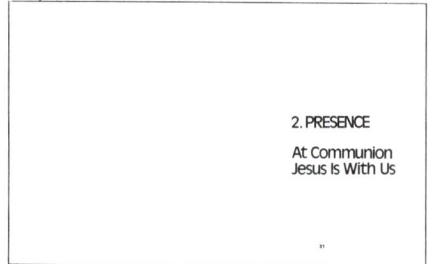

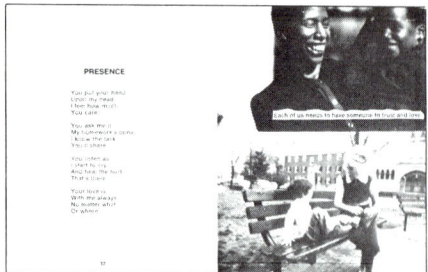

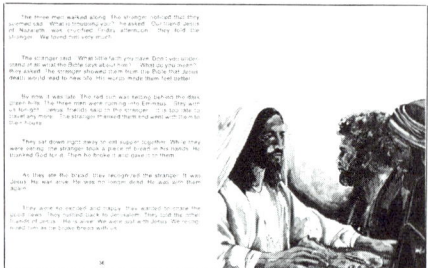

Point out that what happens at the Eucharist is just what happened in this story. Jesus is just as present with us at Communion as he was with his two friends at Emmaus. We come to know that he is with us as we come together to listen to the Scriptures and to eat the bread Jesus gives us. He is with us also along the way of life as he was with his two friends. He is with us to take away our sadness and help us to be happy.

4. EXPLORE SIGNS OF JESUS' PRESENCE

Talk briefly about how we know Jesus is with us. *Tell your family that we find out very much in the same way that the two disciples discovered he was with them—through people who, like the traveler, care enough to be with us, and through special signs, like those that Jesus used at Emmaus and along the way.* Use the Child's Book as you wish in order to show the special signs of Jesus' presence with us at the Eucharist and at all times and places. Talk about them to the extent that there is interest. Your child can do the drawing and pasting at another time.

5. ENJOY BEING WITH EACH OTHER

Then just relax. You have covered the essentials. At another time during the week you can reinforce the learnings with your First Communion child. Now just relax and enjoy each other's presence for as long a time as is convenient.

Really try to *be with* your family as you enjoy the picnic, walk, or other experience you selected. Don't force any conversation about what you have been learning together. But if your family shows interest in talking more about any of the topics, don't hesitate to talk more with them. *More important at this point is really enjoying each other's presence.*

6. PRAY AND SING

Afterward take just a moment or two to recall Jesus' presence in prayer and song. Pray aloud Psalm 23. Point out that the psalm says that Jesus, the, Shepherd, is with us in *daily life* (resting, leading, giving new life, guiding, comforting, strengthening) and at *Communion* (table of food).

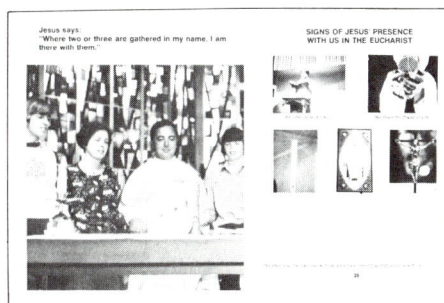

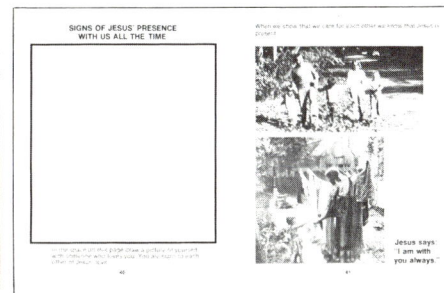

If at all possible, sing together the beautiful song "Hide Me." Use the record to help you learn it and then sing along with it. The singing can be a delightful way of ending what hopefully was a good time together.

WHAT TO DO DURING THE WEEK

To continue informally the preparation for First Communion begun during your picnic, walk and snack, or popcorn eating, you might do a few things like these:

1. Take time with your child sometime during the week to go over the material in the Child's Book. The blank spaces could then be filled in by drawing or pasting signs of Jesus' presence. You might want your child to memorize a summary of what you learned together, using the questions and answers on page 110. Questions 4-7 relate to this session. They are:

(4) How is Jesus with us in Communion?
In Communion Jesus is with us as a friend who shares a meal with us. He is as present to us in Communion as he was to the apostles at the Last Supper, or at the breakfast at the seashore, or at the house in Emmaus. He is with us in the people who gather for Communion and in the signs of bread and wine.

(5) Is Jesus with us only at Communion?
No. Jesus is with us all the time, wherever we may be. He is with us in a special way at Communion. Communion is a celebration of his presence with us always.

(6) What are some signs of Jesus' presence with us always?
The best signs of Jesus' presence with us always are people who love us. Other signs are anyone or anything that helps us to grow as free, creative, caring persons. Special signs of Jesus' presence are people who are poor or are in need. Still other signs are everything that is good or beautiful in the world.

(7) What are some signs of Jesus' presence with us in Communion?
The best sign of Jesus' presence with us at Communion is the love of the people who celebrate the Eucharist with us. Special signs are the bread and wine, and the Bible. Other signs are the altar, the burning candle, the crucifix, and pictures or statues of Jesus.

2. Read with your child a book that brings out the importance of another's presence—for example:
CROW BOY by Taro Yashima (New York: Viking-Penguin, 1955)

LOUIE by Ezra Jack Keats (New York: Greenwillow books—Division of William Morrow, 1975)

ANNIE AND THE OLD ONE by Miska Miles (Boston: Little, Brown, 1971)

3.   Have your child learn by heart the words of Jesus on pages 38 and 41. These could be woven into any prayer times you have as a family, such as at mealtime or bedtime.

4.   Copy out, or help your child copy out, Psalm 23. Hang it somewhere where the whole family can see it. Or buy a plaque with Psalm 23 (available at most religious goods stores) and give it as a present to your child.

5.   Learn the song "Hide Me" by heart. Sing it with your child occasionally during the week, perhaps each evening at supper or dinner. Or, play the recording at meals or other times during the week.

6.   Make a book with your child that says: "Presence is . . . ." Search through magazines and newspapers for pictures that illustrate presence or stories that tell about the difference that someone's presence made in either a good or bad situation.

7.   Ask your child to write a story or a poem about "presence-and-Communion" as he or she understands it.

BACKGROUND NOTES

Real Presence

Jesus is present with us in the Eucharist. This is the traditional belief of Catholics and many other Christian churches. Today there is growing agreement among Christians that Jesus' eucharistic presence is something very real. It is important to help the child approaching Communion for the first time to grow in awareness of Jesus' presence with us through this sacrament.

Experiencing Presence

A child's sense of Jesus' presence is rooted in the soil of daily experience. Without experiences of the presence of others with them in love and trust, children are unable to grasp the reality of Jesus' presence in the Eucharist or in life.

So an important part of First Communion preparation is to *be with* the children in ways that enable

2. PRESENCE

At Communion
Jesus Is With Us

them to *feel* your presence as an important part of their lives. As the poem suggests, feeling someone's presence is experienced through the care, the sharing, the compassion and the love that is communicated through physical signs. Mere physical presence alone is not enough.

A Walk with a Traveler

It was that kind of caring presence that the two disheartened disciples of Jesus experienced as they walked toward Emmaus with a traveler they met along the way. The traveler walked with them as a sensitive, caring person. He sensed their sadness. He listened to them as they shared their pain. He communicated a sense of understanding, care and compassion. His presence and his words began to revive their spirits.

They recognized the traveler as Jesus when, as also happened at the Last Supper, he broke bread and shared it with them. The language of Luke's description of the meal at Emmaus is almost exactly the same as he used to describe what Jesus did at the Last Supper. It is basically the same as is still used at Mass. Almost the same words and actions were used by the early Christian communities as they celebrated the Eucharist in their homes.

Words and Food

Luke's story in face reflects the format of those early celebrations. It reveals two of the major ways the Church has recognized Jesus' presence with them along the way of life: the word of God and the Bread of Life. The two disciples began to sense Jesus' presence as he explained the Scriptures to them. They finally recognized him in the "breaking of the bread."

The present-day celebration of the Eucharist preserves this ancient structure. The Mass is composed of the liturgy of the word and the liturgy of the Eucharist. Jesus' real presence is recognized in the word of God which is read and preached and in the Bread of Life which is shared.

Sacred Signs

Actually the primary sign of Jesus' presence with us in the Eucharist is the people who gather to express

Note: Source of the story: Luke 24:13-35

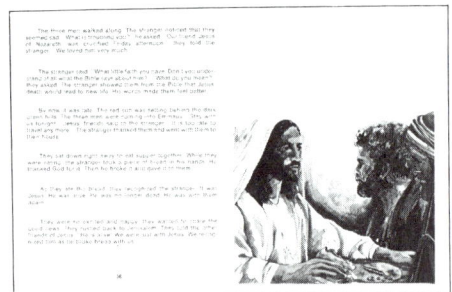

28

their faith and love. It is the community of believers gathered in Jesus' name to worship the Father and to support one another that most movingly reveals Jesus' presence. He suggested this when he pointed out that he was present wherever two or three came together in his name. Christian tradition has expressed the same belief by calling the Church "the body of Christ." Vatican Council II teaches that when the people sing and pray at Mass, Christ is present.

What the worshiping community *does* together reveals Jesus' presence in its midst. Two sacred are particularly important as the Emmaus story suggests: the proclaiming of God's word and eating the Bread of Life. Within these sacred actions certain objects find their special meaning, particularly the Bible and the bread and wine (the "eucharistic species").

For several centuries Roman Catholics centered their attention almost exclusively on the bread and wine. They were seen as the chief signs of Jesus' real presence at Mass. In recent years, since Vatican Council II, the Church has tried to balance the overemphasis on the eucharistic species. This is done, not by denying their importance as signs of Jesus' real presence, but by viewing them in the perspective of other equally traditional signs of his presence.

A more balanced approach is to see the signs of Jesus' presence in the Eucharist first of all in the community itself. Its actions of proclaiming God's word and eating the Bread of Life particularly reveal Jesus' presence. So do the community's singing, praying, reconciling and offering. It is in relation to these actions of faith and love by the community at worship that the bread and wine find their special significance, as does the Bible. The altar and other artistic symbols are secondary but helpful signs of Jesus' presence.

Secular Signs

It is not that Jesus is present with us only at the eucharistic meal. Quite the contrary. In celebrating his presence with us then, we come to realize and celebrate the fact that he is with us all the time.

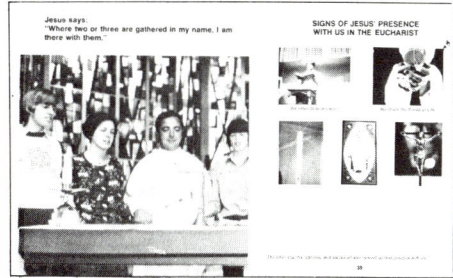

Note: Source of quote: Matthew 18:20

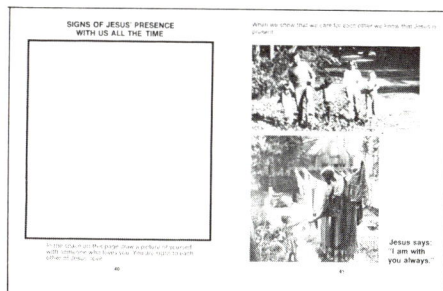

Note: Source of quote: Matthew 28:20

29

That is what he promised in what Matthew records as Jesus' final words, "I am with you always." Signs of Jesus' presence are all around us. Paul and John hinted that the beauties and mysteries of life might reveal his presence. Christian tradition led millions of believers to look for signs of Christ's presence in all that they experience.

Scripture and tradition unite in pointing to special signs of his daily presence: love, peace, joy, patience, kindness, generosity, chastity (Gal. 5:22-23). The normal way we experience the healing, challenging, enlivening presence of Jesus with us in daily life is through people who relate to us with respect, care and compassion. People who love us are the normal signs of the presence of the risen Lord and his Spirit with us all the time.

Prayer and Song

From the earliest Christian communities down through the centuries, faith in the real presence of Jesus has been expressed in prayer and song. Psalm 23, the Good Shepherd psalm, was early used at eucharistic celebrations to speak of the presence of the risen Lord with his people in the Eucharist and in all life's experiences. That same trust is echoed in the song "Hide Me" which sees the presence of Christ as a source of light, peace, freedom and guidance.

3. UNITY
At Communion We Are United
With Jesus and His Friends

JUST A THOUGHT

Four children were playing on the playground. There was an argument. Three turned against one and began screaming at him. They would not let him play with them any longer. He yelled back as he walked away. Tears rolled down his cheeks as he cried. He felt angry and alone.

Loneliness is something we all experience, and it is painful, particularly if we feel cut off, separated from others, or if we feel that no one cares about us, that we belong to no one. It is good at times to be alone, but it is never good to be lonely.

A sense of belonging is necessary to our happiness, even to our physical well-being. A twentieth-century philosopher expressed the condition perfectly when he wrote, "No man is an island." We become most ourselves through union with others. Few things are as important for a child as to *feel* and *be* part of at least a few people who love him or her.

First Communion preparation provides a ready-made chance to help your child and your whole family feel more at one, because Communion is precisely about unity. Unity is what Jesus prayed for at the Last Supper. Paul wrote not long after that those who share the same eucharistic bread become one body. The Church today describes the Eucharist simply as a "sacrament of unity."

Ideal preparation for First Communion involves efforts to grow in unity. When the whole family joins in to help a child prepare for First Communion, a closer relationship can develop. Sometimes a sense of how good it was to be together at that time will be appreciated much later. That's all right! Communion is meant to celebrate and reveal the unity you already have and to deepen and expand it. First Communion preparation shares in that process of becoming more unified.

In this session you have a chance to help your child learn that Communion is about unity, about belonging. More important, you and the whole family can help him or her experience that unity and belonging.

A PLAN OF ACTION

Goal
To help your child to:
(1) experience a sense of belonging and unity within the family;
(2) learn that Communion is about unity—at the Eucharist and in daily life.

Experience
A special family breakfast, or another setting of your own choice.
Select a setting that will encourage a feeling of unity and belonging as you learn together. A special family breakfast is outlined in the plan because the Gospel story for this session is about a breakfast with Jesus. Follow the plan without the meal if you prefer.

Materials
(1) The Child's Book.
(2) The record, and record player.
(3) Special breakfast foods.

Preparations
(1) Read the plan below and adapt it to your family's style. See also the Background Notes on pages 42-45.
(2) Prepare the table and food with extra care to make it special.

Summary
(a) Using the Child's Book, talk together about unity and Communion.
(b) Enjoy being together.
(c) Pray and sing, using the Child's Book and record.

Directions

1. SHARE YOUR PLAN
When the family has come together in a designated place, explain that you are going to continue First Communion preparation with a special breakfast. Add that since you can be together so seldom for breakfast, you thought a special breakfast together might be nice. If there are particular foods the fam-

3. UNITY

At Communion
We Are United
with Jesus
and His Friends

ily likes, tell them that these are what you are having after you learn more about Communion together.

2. TALK ABOUT BEING TOGETHER
Then reflect on what *being together* means, about how good it is to belong.

By way of contrast, you might begin by telling stories of times when you were lonely or left out or overlooked. Let the whole family join in with experiences of being lonely and descriptions of how it feels to be out of touch with others. Then talk about how it feels being together with others, belonging to a group, and about what a difference it makes to feel united with others—such as when they can bring their friends in for a cold drink or cookies, or when friends like them so much they invite them to go with them and their families on a trip or to dinner or to a movie, or when someone in their class is having a birthday party and wants them to come.

Use the Child's Book as a help to sharing about unity. The title of this third session suggests that Communion is about unity.

In the poem and the pictures your child and others in the family may find experiences that remind them of their own experiences. The poem might be read aloud and talked about. Talk together about belonging and unity as long as everyone is interested.

3. TALK ABOUT GOSPEL STORY
Look together at the pictures in the Child's Book of the seashore breakfast. Your child or others in the family may be able to tell the story from the picture. Or you might tell the story or read it from the book as the others continue to look at the picture. Focus attention more on the breakfast itself than on the catching of the fish.

As you talk together about the story, help your child sense from the pictures and story how happy the disciples must have been to be with Jesus and with each other on this occasion. They were together because they were all friends of Jesus. They belonged to each other because they belonged to him.

3. UNITY

At Communion
We Are United
with Jesus
and His Friends

TOGETHER

A Story of Jesus and His Friends,
as Told by John.

33

Point out how similar this breakfast scene is to Communion. There are friends sharing a meal with Jesus. There is bread which Jesus gives to his friends to eat. (The fish was a common early Christian symbol of Jesus, too.) Jesus' actions in breaking and giving them the bread are almost the same as those of the priest at Communion.

The seashore breakfast is really a story about the Eucharist. From it we can learn that Communion is about community. It is about being together as friends because of a friendship with Jesus. Union with Jesus involves union with all who are united with him.

4. EXPLORE SYMBOLS OF UNITY

You might look briefly together at pages 54-55 in the Child's Book to reinforce the point that Communion is about unity.

The two symbols suggest that through Communion many (grains of wheat; people) become one (loaf of bread; body). They both are about the bread of Communion.

The pictures on the next pages suggest that Communion is not just about unity at Mass but also about community at home, at work, at school, at play. The unity experienced at Communion builds on and builds up our sense of togetherness in daily life. Read and talk about the two brief quotes.

Communion is about unity with Jesus and with one another, at Mass and in the rest of life.

5. ENJOY THE SPECIAL BREAKFAST

By now you have learned together an extremely important lesson about Communion, so relax and eat. Simply enjoy being together as you eat and talk. Do simple things to express your belonging as a family. For example, hold hands and say grace or sing a favorite song.

Talk about the Gospel story and Communion only if they come up spontaneously in your conversation. *More important at this point is the experience of how good it is to be together as a family.*

6. PRAY AND SING

As the meal draws to an end, sum everything up in a prayer and a song.

Pray together the prayer Jesus gave us. It calls God *our* Father, suggesting that we are all united as brothers and sisters. Hold hands with each other as you pray. If you feel comfortable doing so, pray with simple gestures.

Then, if at all possible, sing the beautiful song, clapping together as you sing. Perhaps sing along with the record, or at least listen to the record. Singing has a way of making people feel united.

As a final gesture of unity, you might hug each other as a sign of peace and harmony.

WHAT TO DO DURING THE WEEK

To continue informally the preparation for First Communion begun at the special breakfast or other setting that you chose, you might do things like these:

(1)   Take a few quiet minutes sometime during the week to go over the session in the Child's Book. This will allow for helpful repetition and provide another opportunity for sharing your own faith and understanding. Question 8 on page 110 is a brief summary of what this session is about. You may want your child to memorize it:

8. What does Communion have to do with other people?
In Communion we are united with Jesus. Communion is a sign of our unity together and a source of still deeper unity.

(2)   Read with your child a piece of children's literature that brings out the value and importance of being with others, of community. Some possibilities are:

STONE SOUP by Marcia Brown (New York: Charles Scribner Sons, 1947)
SWIMMY by Leo Lionni (New York: Random House, 1963)
MAXIE by Mildred Kantrowitz (New York: Parents' Magazine Press, 1970)

(3)   Have your child copy and draw a picture to accompany the quotation from Psalm 133 on page 57. Hang it in a place where the whole family can see it. Perhaps everyone could learn it and use it as a meal or bedtime prayer all week.

(4)   Help your child learn the poem on page 48. Talk with him or her about it once or twice during the week.

(5)   Ask your child to draw a picture of the Gospel story of Jesus eating breakfast with his friends on the seashore—as he or she imagines the event. Display it for all to see and comment on during the week. Or, you might, as a family, create a mural of the event.

(6)   The whole family might learn the song and sing it sometime each day during the week.

(7)   Suggest that your child make a "Notes About Being Together" book in which he or she writes stories of good times enjoyed with family or friends, collects autographs of people he or she enjoys being with, and pastes in pictures that show people playing or working together, praying or singing together.

BACKGROUND NOTES

Community

Unity is what the Eucharist is basically all about. It is what Jesus prayed for at the Last Supper. It is what St. Thomas Aquinas in the Middle Ages taught to be the fundamental reality of the Eucharist. The Second Vatican Council defines the Eucharist as a "sacrament of love, a sign of unity, a bond of charity."

Communion is a *sign* of our union with each other and with Jesus Christ who is present with us. It is also a *source* of ever deeper communion with him and with each other.

Being With

Community around the altar does not just happen. It finds its roots in common, everyday experiences of being with others. That is why an important part of First Communion preparation is helping the children experience a sense of being with others. One of the tragedies of modern living is that so many people, including children, feel alone, separated from others. Preparation for First Communion should include rich experiences of being with others—family, friends, other children and adults in the parish community. The children are part of a

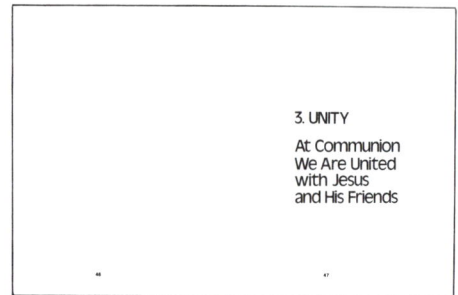

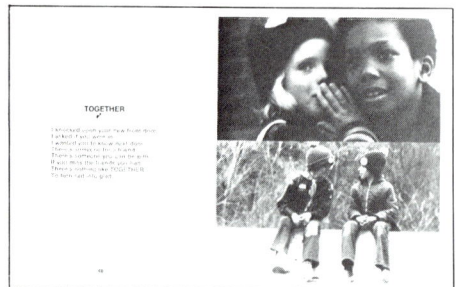

3. UNITY

At Communion
We Are United
with Jesus
and His Friends

TOGETHER

group of people. If some—better yet, all—of these people really care for them, for one another, and for Jesus Christ and his work, Communion has a chance of being an honest sign of genuine closeness and a source of still deeper unity. To receive the "body of Christ" in Communion is intimately related to becoming the "body of Christ" in reality.

Around a Charcoal Fire

The Gospels tell us in symbols and word pictures that to be united with the risen Christ means to be united with others who know and love him. The Last Supper stories show us a gathering of friends whose friendship centered in their love for Jesus. The two disciples, having recognized Jesus as they broke bread with him at Emmaus, immediately got up and returned to the community of Jesus' disciples in Jerusalem.

An even more charming story tells of Jesus cooking breakfast for his disciples. They were hungry and tired after a luckless night of fishing. They were delighted to be with Jesus again. The Gospel picture of the seven disciples sitting on the seashore around a charcoal fire sharing a meal of bread and fish with Jesus is a portrait of the Church sharing the Eucharist.

A Meal of Friendship

Fish and bread were symbols of the risen Christ in the early Christian communities. They were common symbols of the Eucharist. The words used in this story to describe Jesus giving the bread to his friends are the same words used of Jesus at the Last Supper and at Emmaus. They are also the same words used from then until now as Christian communities celebrated the Eucharist.

This story warmly portrays a shared meal that builds upon and builds up a friendship between those who eat together. It shows too that what holds them together is a shared knowledge and love of Jesus Christ. Communion with him involves community among themselves.

Communion Means Community

Paul insisted on this to the Corinthian community which was split into many factions. He stressed that

Note: source of story: John 21:1-14

37

those who shared the one eucharistic bread actually became one body. One of the earliest texts of a eucharistic prayer we have, after the New Testament, makes the same point with somewhat different symbolism. Grains of wheat grow scattered in the fields and grapes grow haphazardly on the vines. They are gathered together to make bread and wine. So the Christians prayed that in like manner those who share the bread and wine may be gathered together into one Church.

It Can Be Fun

So as we help the children to prepare for their First Communion a major goal should be to help them sense something of the joy and security that comes from being part of a caring community. The result should be that they sense that receiving Communion has something to do with being with others who also are with Jesus.

Psalm 133 expresses how good it is, and how much fun it can be, when people live together as friends. Such unity is a basic theme of the Hebrew Scriptures. The early Christians found Psalm 133 to be an appropriate prayer-song for use at the Eucharist. At the Last Supper Jesus prayed urgently that his friends be united with each other with the same kind of friendship that bound him to each of them. So it is not surprising that the Church so closely links Communion with community.

A Common Father

The Communion rite at Mass begins with everyone praying together the very prayer Jesus himself taught us. The Our Father is the prayer of persons who know themselves as brothers and sisters. God is *our* Father. The Lord's Prayer is *the* prayer of the family of Christ—all those who are united with each other in being united with him. From the earliest days of the Church, the Our Father has been linked with the celebration of the Eucharist, with Holy Communion.

To be so closely united is something to sing about. The song simply does that, singing of the bonds of unity that tie us together. Being together is what Communion is all about.

Note: source of quotes: 1) *Didache,* or *The Teaching of the Twelve Apostles,* writing before 150 A.D., perhaps much earlier. 2) 1 Cor. 10:17

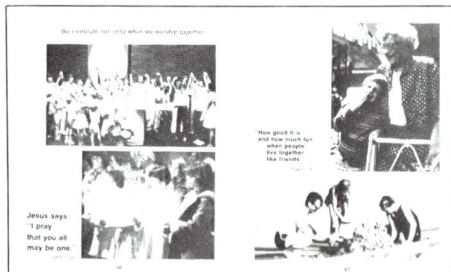

Note: Source of quote: John 17:20

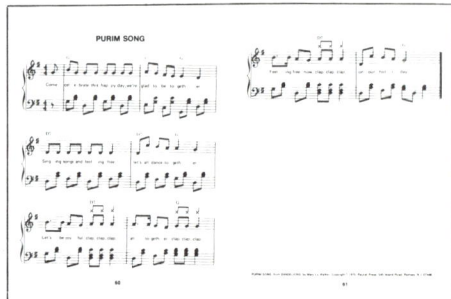

4. FOOD
At Communion Jesus
Is the Bread of Life For Us

JUST A THOUGHT

"Can I have a cookie, Dad?" "I'm hungry. When are we going to eat?" "I'm thirsty. I need a drink." "Buy me some candy, *please.*"

Food is never far from the mind of children. Some days they seem to be perpetually hungry—until dinner time when they bolt down what they like and want to run off. Within an hour they may be asking for something more to eat or drink.

Talking about food and eating together are part of First Communion preparation because Communion is received as food. Yet it is not just ordinary food. Going to Communion is not just like going to McDonald's, Gino's or Roy Rogers'. An important prerequisite for your child receiving Communion is that he or she knows that the eucharistic food is not ordinary food.

The difference does not have to do with how it looks or tastes. The wine looks and tastes like wine. The bread used in many parishes looks and tastes more like regular bread than do the round white hosts. The difference is that what is eaten and drunk at Communion is done so in a community worship setting. It is clearly related to one's faith. The eucharistic bread and wine are identified with Jesus himself in this community service.

You can help your child to accept and believe this. The mystery of it all transcends the learning process. The lesson uses a Gospel story to bring out the difference. In the story Jesus feeds a hungry crowd regular food, bread and fish. The next day he promises them a more important food, the Bread of Life. He then tells them that he is the Bread of Life.

At Communion your child will receive the Bread of Life. He will receive Jesus. The bread and wine may look and taste like regular bread and wine, but they are more than ordinary food. They are the Bread of Life, which is Jesus himself.

PLAN OF ACTION

Goal
To help your child to:
(1) appreciate the gift of food and its importance for life;
(2) believe that the food received in Communion is more than ordinary food;
(3) believe that the bread and wine of Communion are identified with Jesus himself, the Bread of Life;
(4) believe that those who eat the Bread of Life are united with Jesus now and will live forever with him.

Experience
A family lunch or another setting which you prefer. Select a setting that will allow for you all to enjoy eating and drinking together as you talk about ordinary food and about the Bread of Life. The plan suggests a family lunch because the Gospel story of the Bread of Life begins with a lunch with Jesus in the country.

Materials
(1) The Child's Book.
(2) Food and drink that is appropriate to the setting.
(3) The record, and record player.

Preparations
(1) Read the plan below and adapt it to your family's style. See also the Background Notes on pages 50-53.
(2) Prepare the table and food with extra care to suggest that this is part of the special preparation for Communion.

Summary
(1) Using the Child's Book, talk together about food and the Bread of Life.
(2) Enjoy eating together.
(3) Pray and sing together, using the Child's Book and record.

Directions

1. SHARE YOUR PLAN
Invite your child and the rest of the family to have

lunch (a snack, picnic, etc., as you wish) together to continue your preparation for First Communion.

2. TALK ABOUT FOOD
Before eating—or while you eat if your prefer—talk together about food and hunger. The Child's Book relates Communion with the word "food" as a reminder that the conversation about food is part of First Communion preparation.

Enjoy the poem and pictures together. Your family may find in the poem some of their favorite foods, or you might talk about what some of them are.

Talk about how it feels to be hungry and how good it is then to have something to eat. With your family, think and talk about how important food is in our lives as well as how good it is. Without food and drink we could not live.

3. TALK ABOUT GOSPEL STORY
As recognition grows about how important food is for life, share the Gospel story about the Bread of Life.

The pictures in the Child's Book show the high points of the story—the multiplication of loaves, and Jesus talking about himself as the Bread of Life. Let your child tell you what the pictures say to him or her. As a family recall as much about the story as you can before reading it.

Then read the story on these pages and talk about it some more. *Point out that Jesus promises another kind of food than ordinary bread and fish. He calls it the Bread of Life. He says that he is the Bread of Life. That is the bread we receive in Communion. It is Jesus himself. If we eat the Bread of Life Jesus promises that we will live with him forever.*

At this point you might ask your child if he or she wants to go to Communion, to receive the Bread of Life. If so, and he or she has some sense that the Communion bread and wine are more than ordinary food, then he or she has the minimum requirements for receiving First Communion.

4. TALK ABOUT ORDINARY FOOD AND THE BREAD OF LIFE

The Child's Book may further help your child see that what is received in Communion is food like other food, but that it is more than ordinary food.

Let him or her describe what might be drawn in the two pictures. The actual drawing can be done later in the week as a reinforcement of what is learned. The picture on page 72 suggests, too, that this is more than an ordinary meal—the praying, singing, silence, and various other signs of Jesus' presence. Point out Jesus' words next to the Communion picture. The Bread of Life received at Communion is Jesus himself.

The pictures on the next page try to make the same point—food, but more than ordinary food. It is for both foods that we pray in the Our Father and for which we thank God at Mass.

5. ENJOY EATING TOGETHER

With that your child has learned all that is necessary for this session. Now it is time to enjoy food together. In a leisurely way eat what you prepared for lunch or for the other setting you chose.

As you eat, you might talk more about the importance of food and drink and how good they are. You might talk more about the Bread of Life, but only if the conversation is natural. It might be better to simply enjoy eating and being together.

6. PRAY AND SING

When the meal is finished, close with a prayer that thanks God for the gift of food. Psalm 104 is a beautiful prayer of thanks. It mentions bread and wine, too.

Then sing the song together. It is a Communion song. Try to sing along with the record, or at least listen to the record. If you are unable to sing or hear the record, at least read the lyrics. They are a simple summary of much of what has been learned so far in the first four sessions.

WHAT TO DO DURING THE WEEK

To continue informally the preparation for First Communion begun at the special lunch or other setting that you chose, you might do things like these:

1. Take a few moments sometime during the week to review with your child what has been considered so far in the Child's Book. On pages 70-71 of the Child's Book have your child draw the pictures of a family meal and the eucharistic meal. For a brief question-answer summary you might want your child to learn Question 9 on page 110:

(9) Why does Jesus call himself the Bread of Life?
Jesus calls himself the Bread of Life because he is as important to our life as food and drink. Jesus brings us new life that never ends.

2. Get some Communion bread and wine from your parish. Let your child taste them on several occasions so that at the actual First Communion they will be familiar. Use the occasion to talk more about the Bread of Life which is Jesus. Also practice the two ways of receiving Communion. Directions are found on pages 114-115 of the Child's Book.

3. Read with your child some poetry about food. Some possibilities are:

"This Is Just to Say" by William Carlos Williams, from *Reflections on a Gift of Watermelon Pickle and Other Modern Verse*, Stephen Dunning, Edward Lueder, and Hugh Smith, eds. (Glenview, Ill.: Scott Foresman, 1966).

"Food" by Marchete Chute, from *On City Streets: An Anthology of Poetry,* Nancy Larrick, ed. (New York: M. Evans & Co., 1968).

"Picnics" by Marchette Chute, from *Around and About* (New York: Dutton, 1955).

4. Make and bake bread with your child. Let him or her help as much as possible. Use the time together to talk more about food and the Bread of Life.

5. The prayer on page 74-75, Psalm 104, could be prayed all week at meals to thank God for the gift of food.

6. At Sunday Mass help your child to notice the words of the priest that are almost exactly like those said by Jesus at the Last Supper, the Emmaus meal, the seashore breakfast, and the multiplication of loaves. Sometimes these words are called words of "consecration" or words of "institution."

7. Suggest that your child write a personal prayer expressing a desire to receive the Bread of Life.

8. If your child likes to make booklets, one might be made illustrating and telling a picture-word story entitled: FOOD IS . . . . Magazines might provide a resource for this activity.

BACKGROUND NOTES

Life-Giving Food

One of the most obvious things about Communion is that it involves eating, and sometimes drinking. Food—even though the amount is small—is an important part of the eucharistic celebration. The presence of Jesus is intimately related with the bread and wine. In fact since the time of the Reformation in the sixteenth century, Catholic theology and practice tended to focus almost exclusively on the "eucharistic species," the bread and wine.

At the Second Vatican Council, the Church Fathers reminded us of other traditional signs of Jesus' eucharistic presence. For example, Jesus is present in the gathering of the people and their actions of proclaiming and hearing God's word, forgiving, praying, singing, offering and eating. He is present, too, in the priest. His presence under the appearances of bread and wine is now seen in relation to these other signs of his presence.

Food Values

The child preparing for First Communion needs to grasp that the Eucharist is a meal. It is a meal shared with Jesus. Therefore it is valuable during First Communion preparation to explore with the children their appreciation of food and its vital importance for life. Simply put, we need food just to live. Our food influences the quality of our health. Bread is the "staff of life."

The Bread of Life

Jesus himself moves from the people's hunger for food to their still deeper hunger for nourishment to unending life. The dramatic story of the feeding of the multitude is told in all four Gospels and is repeated with variations a second time in two of them. Only John adds the long discourse on the Bread of Life.

After feeding the 5,000 men, plus women and children, with five barley loaves and two fishes, Jesus challenged the people to deal with that deeper

Note: Source of story: John 6:1-15, 25-59 see also Mark 6:30-44 and 8:1-10 Matthew 14:13-21 and 15:32-39 Luke 9:10-17

hunger. He identified himself with the Bread of Life given by the Father so that people could live more fully and forever. Jesus firmly states, despite the people's skepticism, that he himself is real food.

Eucharistic Bread
The story as told in the Gospels clearly reflects the experience of the early Christian communities with the "breaking of bread" or Eucharist. John's language describing Jesus taking bread, blessing it, and giving it to the people is the same language used by Jesus at the Last Supper. It is the same language used in the eucharistic celebration from the earliest days of Christianity down to today. The bread of the Eucharist is the Bread of Life. It is Jesus himself.

No Ordinary Food
Thus children preparing for First Communion do well to learn that Communion involves eating food and also drinking at times. But they need to appreciate that the eucharistic bread and wine are not ordinary food. They need not learn highly abstract concepts like "transubstantiation." They do, however, need to become aware that the bread and wine are somehow identified with Jesus.

According to John, Jesus says, "I am the Bread of Life." The Church's liturgy speaks of "the Bread of Life." In using these terms we suggest to the children that Jesus is food for our lives, but food in a deeper sense than the food needed to keep us physically alive. The bread received in Communion is more than ordinary bread. It is the Bread of Life. It is Jesus Christ.

Thanks and Praise
At the community meal that is the Mass we thank God for all of creation, particularly for bread and wine and all foods and drinks. We thank and praise God even more for the Bread of Life and the cup of salvation which nourish the deepest hunger of our lives. It is for both these foods that we pray in the Our Father, "Give us this day our daily bread." We need food and drink, bread and wine for nourishment and rejoicing. Even more we need the nourishment of Jesus' presence with us as the Bread of Life and the cup of salvation.

Note: Source of quote: John 6:48

A Prayer and a Song

The children are led in praying one of the beautiful psalms from the Hebrew Scriptures. It is a song in praise of God for creation, and in particular for food and drink. At the Eucharist we gather together to praise and thank God for food and for all the good things of creation that help us to live healthily and happily. We praise and thank him in particular for the gift of Jesus Christ as our food for unending life. At Communion we eat the Bread of Life which Jesus identifies with himself.

The gift of the Bread of Life is something to sing about. Children preparing for their First Communion have a right to share some of the joy of partaking of this food for the first time. Without Jesus they, and we, cannot live fruitful Christian lives any more than we can sustain our health without basic foods and drinks. Part of First Communion preparation is fostering their hunger or desire for the Bread of Life.

5. GIFT
At Communion
Jesus Gives Us Himself

JUST A THOUGHT

Nancy Lopez, the famous golfer, ascribes a great deal of her success to her parents' self-sacrifice. They did without many things so that she could develop her golfing skills. They gave of themselves for her.

Harry and Jane do something similar for their two sons. Every afternoon or evening the two of them spend a half hour or hour with their two boys. Jane and Harry both work and have frequent political and social obligations at night. But that time for being with their children is almost sacred. It is one way they give themselves to their two sons and give them an opportunity to return the gift.

Often the best gifts are *personal* ones. They are usually the hardest to give, even if they involve more fun and satisfaction than just giving things as gifts. Children are able to feel the difference between gifts that express self-giving and gifts that do not.

Our personal patterns of giving ourselves are helpful to our understanding of Jesus' gift of himself to us. We believe that Jesus gives us himself in Communion, so consideration of self-giving is an important part of your child's First Communion preparation.

Jesus' gift of himself in Communion brings us into contact with his total self-gift on the cross. What he did then for us, he does now in the Eucharist. Risen from death and alive with new life, he gives himself.

His self-gift suggests how much he loves us. He told his friends at the Last Supper that no greater love exists than to give oneself, one's life, for one's friends. In this session you can help your child know in a deeper way that Jesus loves him or her so much that he gives himself, his life, for each of us.

What this means becomes more real for your children at those times when they realize how much your love for them causes you to give of yourself.

A PLAN OF ACTION

Goal
To help your child to:
(1) experience the family's love through their "gifts of self";
(2) believe Jesus loves us so much that he gives us himself in Communion.

Experience
A family prayer session, or another setting of your own choice.
Select a setting that will encourage the experience of mutual self-giving. The plan suggests a simple prayer session together centering on self-giving. You may prefer a party setting with the giving of gifts.

Materials
(1) The Child's Book.
(2) A crucifix, wrapped as a gift.
(3) A candle and matches.
(4) The record, and record player.

Preparations
(1) Read the plan below and adapt it to suit your family's style. See also the Background Notes on pages 60-62.
(2) Have all members of the family, beforehand, decide on some practical way in which they might show their love for the First Communion child by giving something of themselves, e.g., an hour with the child doing anything he or she wants, a lunch or snack out alone with you, an hour or two of time to help with a project. All family members write down their "gift of self" and put it in a decorated envelope.

Summary
(a) Using the Child's Book, share and talk about self-giving and "gifts of self."
(b) Celebrate Jesus' gift of self with Child's Book, gift crucifix, and candle.
(c) Pray and sing, using the Child's Book and record.
(d) Have a snack or party food at home or go out to a favorite haunt for pizza or ice cream or hamburgers and french fries.

Directions

1. SHARE YOUR PLAN
Gather near a table covered with a good tablecloth and with the prepared envelopes, the candle and matches, and the gift-wrapped crucifix decoratively arranged on it.

Indicate that as part of the First Communion preparation the whole family is going to spend a few minutes together praying. Show everyone the words, "At Communion Jesus Gives Us Himself." That is what you will be talking and praying about.

2. PRAY AND SING
Stand together in a circle holding hands or with your arms around each other. Begin with a song you all like, or with the song at the end of this session in the Child's Book and on the record. Sing it, sing along with the record, or just listen to it.

Pray together briefly in any way you are comfortable—maybe just praying the "Our Father" or one of the other prayers you have learned or the prayer for this session in the Child's Book. Or make up a prayer that fits the idea of self-giving, or spend a minute of silence thinking of Jesus' presence with you.

3. TALK ABOUT GIFT GIVING
Then sit down around the table and share among yourselves your thoughts about gifts and gift-giving. Use the poem and picture in the Child's Book to suggest what it means to give not just things but to give yourself. The poem and pictures may trigger memories or experiences each of you has had with self-giving. Talk about what a difference it makes when people give of themselves to another, rather than giving "thing" gifts.

4. GIVE GIFTS OF SELF
Give the Communion child the envelopes, one by one, containing the gifts of self. Take time for all to appreciate the practical ways of self-giving that are revealed. Make plans together as to when the gifts

5. GIFT

At Communion
Jesus
Gives Us Himself

I WONDER IF
THE GIFT OF ME

will be given—sometime before the First Communion date. Reflect more on self-giving and how it shows love. Point out how self-giving, self-sacrificing for another, is a sign of love.

5. TALK ABOUT JESUS' GIFT OF HIMSELF

Then talk about Jesus' gift of himself. Stand up again, as at Mass, to hear the Gospel read. Read, or let someone else in the family read, the adapted version of the Gospel from your child's book on pages 82-85. When the reading is finished say, "This is the Gospel of the Lord," to which all answer, as is done at Mass, "Praise to you, Lord Jesus Christ."

Then sit down again and look together at the pictures of the story. Let your child and others retell the Gospel story using the pictures.

Talk together about the story. *Focus on Jesus' words of love for his friends. He says that he is willing to give his life for them. He gives them himself as the Bread of Life at the Last Supper. It was a sign of his great love, a love that led him to give himself totally on the cross.*

6. GIVE CRUCIFIX AS GIFT

Then give your child the crucifix you have wrapped as a gift. Let him or her look at it and show it to all present. Talk about how it reminds us of Jesus' great love for us, a love that led him to give his life for us. Each might then kiss the crucifix as a sign of appreciation.

If it can be worn, help your child put it on. If not, have your child place it on a stand prepared beforehand for it, preferably beside or in front of the candle.

7. TALK ABOUT JESUS' RESURRECTION

Then look at the art on pages 86-87 of the Child's Book. Comment that Christians believe that Jesus' love is even greater than death. He rose from death to be with us and give himself to us. He is alive and with us right now.

Light the candle as a sign of Jesus' presence. Recall the Easter candle in church, the baptismal candle your child may still have, and the lighted candles at the eucharistic celebration and before the tabernacle. They all remind us that Jesus is risen. He is alive and with us.

Invite all to be very still for a moment and look at the candle, thinking of Jesus who is with you. You might say together: "Christ has died, Christ is risen, Christ will come again."

8. TALK ABOUT COMMUNION
Then look together at the illustration on pages 88-89 in your child's book. *Point out that Jesus gives himself to us at Communion just as he gave himself to his disciples at the Last Supper. But at Communion he gives us himself through the hands and words of the priest or minister of the Eucharist. He gives himself to us because he loves us.*

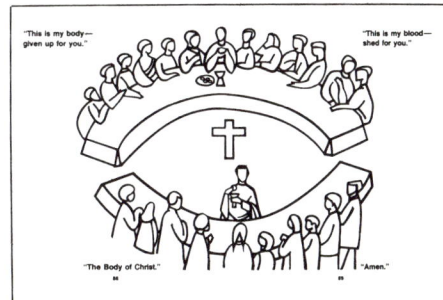

9. PRAY AND/OR SING
End the prayer session with another prayer and song. The prayer in the Child's Book on pages 90-91 is a prayer of thanksgiving for Jesus' gift of himself and for all God's gifts. Pray it all together, perhaps with each of you taking one verse, one after another. It is a prayer prayed at the liturgy by Catholics of the Byzantine rite.

Then sing together the song on page 92. It is a very brief blessing song recalling Jesus' presence with us today as the giver of all good gifts. Sing along with the song on the record if you find that helpful, or just listen to it on the record. Blow out the candle.

10. ENJOY A SNACK
After praying together, enjoy a snack together—pizza, popcorn, ice cream or some other family favorite. Or go out for a surprise treat. It can be a way of giving yourselves to each other as well as giving yourselves a surprise gift. *If possible,* do something festive.

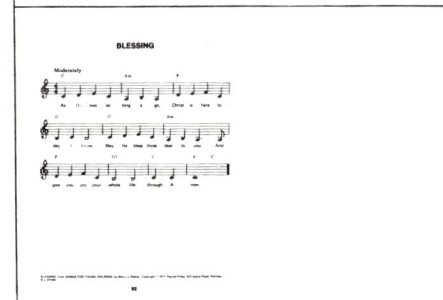

WHAT TO DO DURING THE WEEK

To continue informally the preparation for First Communion begun at the prayer time or however you chose to have the session, you might do things like these:

1.   Take time to go over the whole session quietly with your child who is preparing for First Communion. It can be a good review and enrichment as well as a fine opportunity to get to know each other better. Parents have repeatedly expressed joy and satisfaction about one-on-one times they have had with a child. On pages 110-111 of the Child's Book you may find Questions #10 and #11 helpful as a summary for your child. They are:

10. What does Jesus give us in Communion?
In Communion Jesus gives us himself. He shares his life with us.

11. Why does Jesus give himself to us in Communion?
Jesus gives himself to us in Communion because he loves us and wants to be with us. He wants us to remember him and his love for us.

2.   Read with your child a piece of children's literature that deals with love that involves self-giving. For example,
● Any of those listed in the section, "What To Do During the Week" for Session 6,   p. 67.
● *Amy's Goose* by Efner Tudor Holmes (New York: Thomas Y. Crowell, 1977).
● *The Giving Gift* by Alma Power-Waters (Bell Books, New York: Farrar, Straus & Cudahy, 1962).
● Fairy tales such as *The Wild Swans* in *A Treasury of the World's Greatest Fairy Tales* (The Danbury Press, a division of Grolier Enterprises, Inc., 1972).
● *Stories About Christian Heroes* (a set of well written stories of people who have given of themselves in extraordinary ways) (Minneapolis, Minn.: Winston, Press, 1977).

Afterward talk together about the story in relation to your child's experience and Jesus' self-giving.

3.   With your child look through magazines or newspapers for stories of people who have given of themselves for others because they loved them. Depending on what you find, talk about it in relation to what you considered during the prayer time together. Then have your child do something creative with it. A poster might be made or a drawing or an ad urging people to be self-giving.

4.   At Sunday Mass help your child notice all the ways in which the cross is recalled. For example: crucifix on altar, perhaps on hosts; cross on steeple, on vestments, perhaps on altar; signs of cross made by priest and by people. Also, notice signs of resurrection, i.e., candles, sanctuary lamp, banners, stained glass windows if there is a representation there. Sometimes there is also a fifteenth station depicting the resurrection.

5.   Have your child learn by heart the prayer from the Byzantine liturgy and the brief prayer of St. Paul. These might be copied out and decorated and then hung where the whole family can see them during the week. They could be prayed at meal time or bedtime.

6.   Help your child decide on some practical act of self-giving to be done during the week.

BACKGROUND NOTES

Gift of Self

Communion is a gift. It is a gift of love. In Communion Jesus gives us himself. That's how much he loves us.

Love is expressed in many ways. We can tell people we love them. We can give them gifts to prove our love. But the greatest gift of love is the gift of oneself to another or for another.

Communion celebrates and accepts this greatest of all gifts, Jesus Christ himself. He gave himself *for* us on the cross in a total act of love. Now, risen from death, alive and with us, he gives himself to us because he loves us.

The heart of the message for children preparing for First Communion is that Jesus loves them so much that he gives them himself.

Daily Self-Giving

From their own experience children may feel the difference between giving gifts and giving themselves. Many children sense the painful difference between receiving gifts from parents and receiving the parents' gift of self in taking time to be with their children to listen and to share. Like the person in the poem, children often sense that "the gift of ME" may mean more to another than the gift of toys.

From this instinctive sense of the love that shows through self-giving the children may come to an intuitive awareness of Jesus' love for them.

In the Shadow of the Cross

How much Jesus loves is discovered on the cross. Knowing the danger he was in from his enemies on the night before he actually died, Jesus told his friends as they shared their last meal with him that there was no love greater than that of giving one's life for one's friends. The next afternoon he did just that. He gave his life for all of us whom he calls his friends.

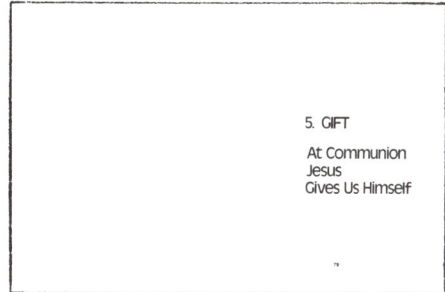

5. GIFT

At Communion
Jesus
Gives Us Himself

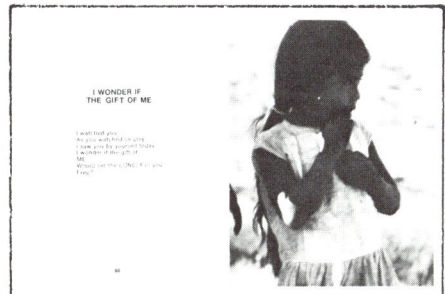

I WONDER IF
THE GIFT OF ME

A Story of Jesus' Gift of Himself
as Told by Luke

Note: Source of Story: Luke 22:14-20

A Gift of Love

The words and actions of the Last Supper are signs of his gift of self. In handing his friends broken bread to eat, he identified it with his "body" and said it would be given up for them. In sharing the cup of wine, he called it his blood, and said it would be shed for them.

The words Jesus used, "my body" and "my blood," say more than we normally mean when we say body and blood in English. In the Bible "body" means my whole person; "blood" means my whole life. Jesus is saying that he is giving himself, his whole life, out of love. In passing the bread and wine to the disciples with those words he gives them himself.

Love Overcomes Death

In theological terms the Church refers to the Mass as a sacrifice or a sacrificial meal. What this means in its most simple and profound sense is that Jesus gives himself totally *to* us and *for* us. He did this by dying on the cross out of love for his Father's work, our salvation. The Father raised him up to new life so that the resurrection power of Jesus' love might be experienced by all people everywhere through His Spirit. Alive and with us, Jesus brings to us the total self-gift of love achieved on the cross. The sacrificial gift of himself on the cross touches us through the sacrament of his love, the Eucharist. Paul expresses the wonder at so great a gift of love.

A Circle of Love

Sometimes pictures can be more meaningful than words. Seeing the Last Supper and Communion visually almost joined in a kind of circle suggests simply that what happens at Communion is very much like what happened at the Last Supper. Like the Last Supper, Communion is a meal with Jesus and his friends. In it Jesus gives himself to us as he gave himself to his disciples.

The Sacrament of the Eucharist makes present the reality of Jesus' loving self-gift on the cross. In Communion we share Jesus' love and accept his gift of himself and his life. What is important for the children receiving their First Communion is to sense that Jesus loves them so much that he gives himself to them at Communion with all the love that led him to die for them on the cross.

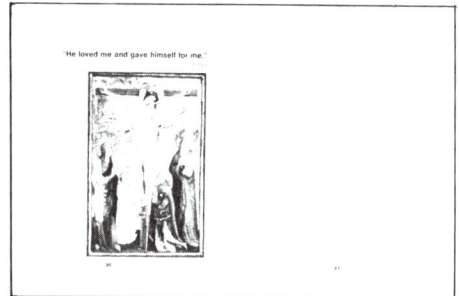

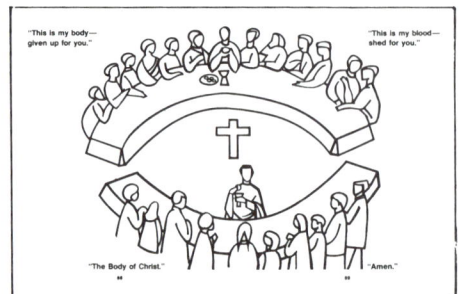

Thanksgiving

Gratitude is a natural response to receiving a gift. Love is a free gift. It cannot be earned. It can only be received with thanks. So Christians from the earliest days have come together to remember Jesus' death and resurrection, to accept his gift of self in Communion, and to thank him. The early name for the Mass and Communion was "Eucharist," which means "thanksgiving" and "praise." Sharing in the Eucharist, celebrating the Eucharist, culminating in Communion, is meant to be an expression of deep thanks for so great a gift. And through that one gift of Jesus, God our Father gives us all other gifts. The Eucharist involves thanks for every gift of God, because all come to us through the one gift of Jesus Christ.

6. SERVICE
At Communion
Jesus Calls Us To Help Others

JUST A THOUGHT

Fourth grade religion class was almost over. It was about selfishness and unselfishness. Ann had been quiet most of the class. Now she mused out loud to herself, obviously struck by something she had never thought about before. "Everybody gives me everything. I have everything I need. I never have to give anything to anybody else. That's not very good for me, is it?"

That was a deep insight for a ten-year-old—one that many adults never learn. The need to give is something we grasp slowly. Actual giving comes still slower.

Learning to give, to help others, is an important part of First Communion preparation. In communion Jesus gives us himself. His love, his gift of himself, invites a return of love, some self-giving on our part. One of the best ways we have of loving him is loving those he loves—other people, especially those in need.

You can help your child become more aware of this by talking together about the example Jesus gave at the Last Supper. He washed his disciple's feet; he served them. Then he told them they were to do to others what he had done to them. They were to serve one another and anyone else in need just as he did. His words and example had greater weight because they knew that his whole life was spent helping others, particularly those most in need.

Even more valuable to your child than talking about helping people is the experience of actually helping someone. An important part of the learning in this session is to plan together and then carry out a project that will help someone in need. Your child, like Ann, deserves the opportunity to learn to give to others as well as to receive. That's part of what Communion is about.

A PLAN OF ACTION

Goal
To help your child to:
(1) share in a project to help someone, and to talk about helping others;
(2) realize that receiving Communion involves a call to help others.

Experience
Quiet time together to plan a project to help someone. Select a setting that will be conducive to working out a plan to help someone as part of the learning about Communion. The plan suggests some quiet time together, with a snack at the end. You may prefer another setting.

Materials
(1) The Child's Book.
(2) The record, and record player.
(3) Food for a snack.

Preparations
(1) Read the plan below and adapt it to your family's style. See also the Background Notes on pages 67-70.
(2) Decide on some person or group genuinely in need whom you as a family can help. Have some concrete ideas in mind as to what you may be able to do.

Summary
(a) Using the Child's Book, talk together about Communion and helping others.
(b) Plan a project to help someone.
(c) Enjoy a snack.
(d) Pray and sing, using the Child's Book and record.

Directions

1. SHARE YOUR PLAN
Indicate that this last session in preparation for Communion will involve helping someone who is in need. Show everyone in the Child's Book the words about Jesus' call to help others.

> 6. SERVICE
>
> At Communion
> Jesus Calls Us
> To Help Others

2. TALK ABOUT HELPING OTHERS

Talk together about helping others. The poem and picture in the Child's Book may spark some ideas or recall some experiences. Discuss how everyone needs help from time to time. Some people have greater needs than others. Be as concrete as possible, using examples that your child and others in the family know about—in your extended family, or the neighborhood, or city, or through the media.

3. TALK ABOUT JESUS' EXAMPLE

Relate those experiences to the example of Jesus. Look together at the pictures of the Gospel story of Jesus washing his disciples' feet. Recall as much of the story as possible from the pictures.

Read the written version of the story if you wish, or tell it in your own words.

Talk about what the story means to all of you. *Point out that Jesus did this at the Last Supper, before "breaking bread" with his disciples. This suggests that Communion has something to do with helping others. Jesus asks those who receive Communion to help others as he did.*

4. TALK ABOUT COMMUNION AND HELPING OTHERS

The Child's Book tries to bring this out with pictures and words. Look at the next pages. Help your child see that it is the same persons receiving Communion in the one picture and helping someone in the other picture. Highlight the fact that those who receive Communion are called by Jesus to help others. His own words express the call.

The pasting and drawing that are called for in the spaces on pages 104-105 can be done later in the week as a reinforcement of what you are learning now. However some consideration might be given to the kinds of pictures that would be good. In this way your child can begin to see himself or herself doing something practical to help someone else.

5. PLAN YOUR HELPING PROJECT

Then work out together a practical plan to help someone in need. It should be a family project that

SHE REACHED OUT HER HAND

A Story of Jesus Serving His Friends
as Told by John

Jesus says: "What I have done for you, you should do for one another."

"Out of love place yourselves at one another's service."

"Put your gifts at the service of one another."

Paste here a picture of someone helping another

Draw here a picture of yourself helping someone

will genuinely help someone. Your child should be able to take an active, even though limited, part in the project.

Identify someone in need. Describe the person's situation and needs. Talk about what you as a family will do. Work out plans that will give everyone in the family something to do in the project. Set a definite date on the calendar prior to the First Communion date for carrying out the plan.

6. ENJOY A SNACK
When you decided what you are going to do and how, relax. You have completed the program of First Communion preparation. Enjoy a snack together—something special that all of you like. Celebrate what you have experienced and learned together over the past weeks of meeting together . You deserve it. You've worked hard and hopefully you have learned much.

7. PRAY AND SING
Conclude your session together with prayer and song. The prayer in the Child's Book on pages 106-107 is perfect for the idea of helping others. Pray it aloud. It is adapted from Jesus' words. You might let each person in the family ask one or more of the questions. Then answer with Jesus' final words.

Sing the song together, if possible using the record. In this way end your preparation on a happy note with song.

WHAT TO DO DURING THE WEEK

To continue informally the preparation for First Communion begun at the planning meeting, you might do things like these:

1. Spend sometime with your child going over what you learned together in the session. Have your child paste a picture of someone helping a person in need and himself or herself helping someone in need on pages 104-105. Then talk together about what the pictures say. You might want to have your child learn the brief summary statements of the lesson— Questions #12 and #13 on page 111.

(12) What does Jesus ask of us at Communion?
At Communion Jesus asks us to open ourselves to him and to all his brothers and sisters. He asks us to love, help and serve one another, especially those most in need.

(13) Why is it good to receive Communion?
It is good to receive Communion to become more closely united with Jesus and with those who love him and us.

2. Carry out the steps you planned to do in your project of helping a needy person or group. As you work at each step, help the children recall that this is related to what Jesus did and to what Communion is all about.

3. Read with your child a piece of children's literature that deals with the value of helping people in need. Some possibilities are:
- *Stone Soup* by Marcia Brown (New York: Scribner, 1947).
- *Tico and the Golden Wings* by Leo Lionni (New York: Pantheon, 1964).
- *Renfroe's Christmas* by Robert Burch (New York: Viking Press, 1968).
- *The Giving Tree* by Shel Silverstein (New York: Harper & Row, 1964).
- *Two Crabs and the Moonlight* by Tohr Yamaguchi (New York: Holt, Rinehart and Winston, 1965).
- *Charlotte's Web* by E. B. White (New York: Harper & Row, 1952).
- *Do You Have the Time, Lydia?* by Evaline Ness (New York: E. P. Dutton, 1974).

Afterward talk about the book in relation to your child's experience and Jesus' example.

4. You all might learn by heart the prayer on pages 106-107. A family project might be to create together an attractive poster or banner with those words. Pictures could be added to further bring out its meaning.

5. Check out all last minute details with the person in the parish in charge of the actual First Communion celebration.

BACKGROUND NOTES

Called To Serve

To receive a gift is an invitation to give in return. To be loved enables and encourages one to love. So it is that the Eucharist is an invitation to give of self as Jesus gives himself. Communion is a sign of love, a call to serve others. To be united with Jesus means to gradually live as he lived, giving of himself to help others. To be united with others means going out to them in response to their needs, helping them carry their burdens.

6. SERVICE

At Communion
Jesus Calls Us
To Help Others

Reaching Out a Hand

Thus an important part of First Communion preparation is to help the children grasp that sharing fully in the Eucharist brings with it a responsibility as well as a privilege. They need to explore their own experiences of helping others and being helped by others. They need to become more aware of people who are hurting, people who need help, people whom they are able to help. The help that children can give may be very small. It may be mostly in terms of helping each other and people close to them, like their parents. But it is important that they become more aware that being a Christian means being open to help anyone who needs help.

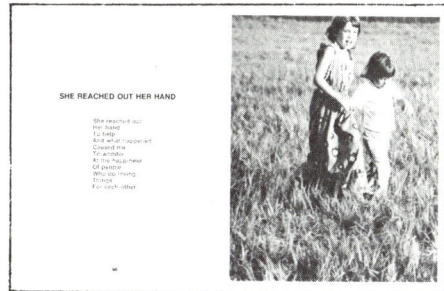

An Example

Jesus makes that point dramatically at the Last Supper. He washes the feet of his disciples, a task normally done at the time by slaves or servants. His act is symbolic. What he does is to be an example to his disciples. They are to become a community of friends dedicated to each other's service. The only power that is to have a place in their communities is the power of love, of mutual service and help.

Jesus' symbolic action of washing his disciples' feet is all the richer in the light of his own life up to that time. What we know of him is that he spent his time going around helping people who most needed help. He was seen typically in the company of the poor, the sick, the sinners. He healed them, instructed them, forgave them, fed them, challenged them, and comforted them. His life was a life of service.

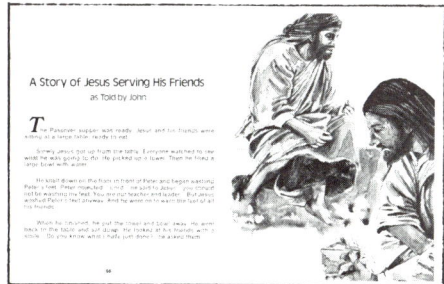

Source of Story: John 13:1-15

Mutual Service

At the Last Supper Jesus tells his friends that they are to live in imitation of him. They are to wash each other's feet, that is, they are to be of mutual service. Then too they are to serve everyone in need, as they saw him do throughout Galilee and Judea.

His example and exhortation to service is given in relation to the meal of friendship they are to enjoy. John tells this story of Jesus washing his disciples' feet, while Mark, Matthew and Luke tell the story of the Last Supper meal. John is suggesting that what the Eucharist is all about in terms of living is mutual love and service. To receive Communion involves

the invitation to build community through concrete acts of love. To receive the body of Christ implies the call to work at building up the body of Christ, the Church.

A Spirit of Love

The children, as they prepare for First Communion, need to be helped to realize that Communion is intimately related to daily life. To receive Jesus' gift of himself means that they are to give of themselves in responding to the needs of others. The love they receive is to be shared with others.

All this is to be shared with them simply. The call to help others should well up out of their awareness of how loved they are. It is not a matter of mere moral exhortation. To appreciate how gifted one is leads more genuinely to gifting others than do promises or threats. We, and the children, are to do for others what Jesus does for us—give of ourselves for others.

Gifted Givers

Children, like all of us, learn this very slowly. They need to be given repeated opportunities to learn that helping others is an essential part of being a member of a Christian community. It is helpful for them to see or experience examples of people responding with care and creativity to persons in need. It is helpful for them to imagine situations in which they do something for others, as well as to recall actual instances when they did help someone. In this way they can learn concretely in terms of their own experience what words like those of Paul actually mean in daily life.

The Final Test

Jesus himself spells out very concretely the implications of being in communion with him. He identifies himself with all who need help—the hungry, strangers, people needing clothes, the sick and lonely, those in prison. To be in communion with Jesus demands being in communion with the needy—in one's own family and neighborhood as well as in the world at large. For Jesus the final test of one's life is how one responds to others in need. He takes such actions, or omissions, personally.

Our children have a right to learn this, simply, in accord with their capacities, as they prepare for their First Communion.

Source of Quotes: 1) Galatians 5:13 2) 1 Peter 4:10

Source of Quote: Matthew 25:37-46